T0383091

# Audit and Trace Log Management

# Audit and Trace Log Management

*Consolidation and Analysis*

## Phillip Q. Maier

Auerbach Publications
Taylor & Francis Group
Boca Raton   New York

Auerbach Publications is an imprint of the
Taylor & Francis Group, an informa business

Published in 2006 by
Auerbach Publications
Taylor & Francis Group
6000 Broken Sound Parkway NW, Suite 300
Boca Raton, FL 33487-2742

International Standard Book Number-10: 0-8493-2725-3 (Hardcover)
International Standard Book Number-13: 978-0-8493-2725-4 (Hardcover)
Library of Congress Card Number 2005057044

### Library of Congress Cataloging-in-Publication Data

Maier, Philip Q.
    Audit and trace log management : consolidation and analysis / Philip Q. Maier.
        p. cm.
    Includes bibliographical references and index.
    ISBN 0-8493-2725-3 (alk. paper)
    1. Computer networks--Security measures. 2. Application logging (Computer science) I. Title.

TK5105.59.M34 2006
005.8--dc22                                                                    2005057044

# Contents

# Foreword

*Audit and Trace Log Management: Consolidation and Analysis* is both a timely and much needed compilation of useful information around a topic that is becoming more and more critical to not only IT professionals and security practitioners, but to many other departments, such as legal, risk, and compliance, as well as auditors and business stakeholders. It is well known and documented that the current body of regulation and legislation will continue to evolve over the next decade, thereby creating an ever-growing and critical need for a cost-effective and efficient audit and monitoring solution.

Security practitioners have always diligently incorporated audit and monitoring into their security management systems, and in support of that, have documented some level of audit and monitoring requirements in their security policies and procedures. However, these new rules are moving the industry and organizations into an entirely new realm, where most of us are ill-prepared to go on our own. This book not only provides an excellent introduction and explanation of the requirements and the problem definition, but it goes further to offer a multidimensional solution set with broad applicability across a wide range of organizations and their needs.

Generally speaking, security solutions and tools tend to lag behind the release of new functionality and technology. Security practitioners are then required to piece together solutions that are ultimately problematic and increasingly cumbersome to support. Even further, the solutions may not really address the problem they are actually initially trying to solve. Implementations can literally take years for larger, more complex enterprises and the solutions may be obsolete before the project is even finished. As the book acknowledges in its currency, the plethora of legislation and regulation has led vendors both to enhance the functionality and inoperability of existing products, as well as to deliver on new auditing and monitoring tools and solutions. This is both the good news and the bad news as the problem suddenly gets larger and harder! The challenge is to choose the right tools and the right solutions unique and specific to your organization's requirements.

The book also delves into the need for sophisticated audit and monitoring tools and processes to support forensic investigations. Although many organizations today outsource the work of forensics because it may not be cost-effective to maintain the skills or the tools in-house, your systems must still provide the logging and audit trail information on the front end of the process. A further challenge then is to not only provide the logging data, but to be able to archive the logs and actually retrieve information back from the process. The book discusses the pitfalls and the challenges of doing this and offers some options and solutions around audit and monitoring in support of forensics.

*Audit and Trace Log Management: Consolidation and Analysis* provides a wealth of information and education in the form of process walkthroughs. These include problem determination, requirements gathering, scope definition, risk assessment, compliance objectives, system design and architecture, implementation and operational challenges, product and solution evaluation, communication plans, project management challenges, and finally making the financial case or determining return on investment (ROI). Utilizing templates, tools, and samples designed and presented to enhance the reader's understandability of the process and the solution set, the author continues to build on the central and core themes of the book. He also includes many diagrams throughout his discussion aiding in a clear understanding of the process and solution recommendations.

Ultimately the readers are provided with a roadmap and a "how to" guideline leading to the successful implementation of a state-of-the-art auditing and monitoring system. Most will want to read it from cover to cover, and also add it to their bookshelves for frequent reference. The most value is derived from the understanding that all projects are different and all organizations change somewhere along their life cycle. Armed with the knowledge from this book, you will be able to champion and guide your organization through a disciplined and well-defined audit and monitoring project. It isn't a stretch to be able to design and implement the system while fulfilling a diverse set of requirements and organizational needs.

At first glance, it would appear that the targeted audience of the book is firstly information security practitioners, but the book also has a more widespread appeal, extending to other business and functional organizations having a stake in the project's success or having a role to play throughout the project's life cycle. Examples of these other organizations include human resources, finance, system and network administrators, auditors, risk and compliance personnel, external auditors and accreditation authorities, IT architects, operational managers, and so on. There is even value to upper management and executives making decisions and approving funding.

Each chapter builds upon the next in an organized and structured fashion providing step-by-step guidance and detailed and thorough explanations. The author uses many illustrations, analogies, and a bit of humor as he leads us through a large and complex set of issues and challenges. He shows us how to understand the drivers leading to the need to implement an audit and monitoring system. At the onset he defines key drivers that are common within our regulatory and legal environment, as well as common to managing risk and security within organizations.

As a peer security practitioner also faced with this dilemma, I appreciate his understanding, knowledge, and experience leading to the realization that this is not a "one size fits all" set of solutions, steps, or phases in comparison to some other IT project such as data center consolidations.

With each chapter, the author continually demonstrates his keen knowledge of the underlying problem we are trying to solve with audit and monitoring. It is clear that he has thought about this problem for a very long time. He understands the well-traveled road that brings us collectively to this resource, seeking knowledge and direction for designing and implementing an audit and monitoring system within our own organizations. Different organizations are all somewhere down the road to solutions in this arena and with this book we can basically step in at any point within the process. It is also a good guideline to assess our own audit and monitoring systems for enhancements and improvements. As readers, we are presented with countless options and information, as well as the tools to "put it all together" for ourselves.

This author is uniquely qualified to speak to this subject. It becomes quickly apparent that he has thought about and struggled with this problem and its resultant challenges for quite some time. He references and discusses countless implementations that he has done over the years as he illustrates the progression of his own thoughts on the subject. He sets out to save us from going down the wrong path in our own implementations and to enable us to benefit from his experience and gathering of knowledge. It is further obvious that he keenly understands that there isn't a "one size fits all" solution set for this problem, but rather, a variety of solutions, based on individual needs and requirements. He discusses a variety of approaches and solutions that include both commercial off-the-shelf (COTS) solutions and internally developed software and solutions. He also addresses combinations of COTS and in-house developed tools as well as combinations and hybrid architectures combining a centralized and decentralized approach.

The author presents no bias with regard to the scope of the project or the ultimate solution set. I feel that each reader will gain enough knowledge, perspective, and insight to independently implement a successful audit and monitoring management system, tailored to each organization's unique set of requirements.

**Lynda L. McGhie, CISSP, CISM**
PCS ISO/Risk Manager
Wells Fargo Bank

# Acknowledgments

The list of people who knowingly or unknowingly contributed to this book is extensive, as many of the insights and much of the knowledge contained herein come from everyone I have worked with on infrastructure security over the past 20 years. The trials and tribulations encountered with trying to make security work in global enterprise systems is immense, and I could not have done it without the support of my peers, staff members, and supportive management. To name a few, I would have to thank Lynda L. McGhie with whom I have worked for nearly all of my 20 years in the security industry; Kent Schwartz who showed me how to intelligently approach security and networking; Jon Bearde who challenged me to deliver real-world solutions; and recently very supportive management, Robyn Strang and Sam Rollins, who ensured I had the resources to apply to my solutions. Staff members who made these architectures work over the years include Andy Bates, Teresa Milly, Connie Sadler, and most recently, Wade Paffile, Jim Farmer, and Patrick Tang. And to those who made all "the words" fall into place I have to thank Jeff Shaw, Laurie Johnson, and Steve Hempler. Finally, I have to express my appreciation for the support and confidence provided me by Kim, Travis, and Cheyenne.

# The Author

**Phillip Q. Maier** is currently the Vice President of the Information Security Emerging Technology & Network group at Inovant, a Visa Solutions Company. He is responsible for overseeing the evaluation, design, and implementation planning for information security technologies at Inovant (a wholly owned subsidiary of Visa USA). The security engineering projects address multiple facets of information protection at Visa both domestically and globally. Key infrastructure security projects include global intrusion detection architecture design and deployment, wireless messaging security internally and externally to the infrastructure, integrated smart-card authentication systems, and custom security log consolidation, correlation, and reporting, as well as a global intranet compartmentalization.

Previously Mr. Maier was the Program Manager of the "Secure Network Initiative" at Lockheed Martin Corp. This initiative was an umbrella program to integrate Lockheed Martin's enterprisewide security projects. He has previously published security papers in Auerbach's *Information Systems Security Journal*, the Electronic Messaging Association's *Security Handbook*, and the *Handbook of Information Security Management*. Mr. Maier is a recognized speaker on security topics at industry forums, academic campuses, and security conferences. He is on the technical advisory board to an emerging security technology company, Packet Motion.

# Chapter 1

# Introduction
# to Audit Logging

The nature of security in the IT sector is constantly evolving. In the last three to six years we have seen an explosive growth in the development of tools for the security trade. These tools were intended to better our abilities to protect our network infrastructures, i.e., to better ensure the overall integrity and security of our infrastructures and in turn to, hopefully, make our lives as IT security professionals easier. In many instances this has been the case. However, it often appears that with the implementation of each new tool not only do we receive new and valuable information, as expected, but in addition we receive a plethora of information. This surplus information poses a serious challenge for those of us on the security team. Not only must we evaluate it, but we must also determine from a security standpoint whether to process it (and how) or simply to understand the information and make intelligent decisions based on it, with respect to the security of the involved network infrastructures.

The security administrators of today may feel like the SETI (Search for Extraterrestrial Intelligence) scientists, who have gathered countless terabytes of radio wave data, and are endlessly sifting through it in an attempt to find intelligible signals that could indicate some signs of intelligent life beyond our world. Similarly, the security administrators of today, thanks to the proliferation of new tools, also encounter volumes of audit data, and although they recognize that it may hold some value to their enterprise (and maybe an indication of intelligent life within their enterprise), they do not yet have the knowledge, or the right tools, to mine the data in a timely manner to uncover its true value.

The proliferation of tools, which has spurred these volumes of audit data, was in direct response to both perceived and real issues and problems raised by enterprise security administrators. This, in turn, drove the vendor community to produce these security toolsets, or to enhance legacy toolsets to fit the enterprise environment. The introduction of new and useful tools was welcomed by security administrators, however, the proliferation of tools and the ensuing outpouring of audit data has, not surprisingly, caused some unexpected challenges to the enterprise security community.

The greatest challenge to those of us who are held responsible for security across the enterprise is to come up with some guiding principles, or an overall "usage strategy" for these tools. We need to reevaluate our use of these tools, not necessarily to "thin the herd," but rather to make better use of what is available and to establish guidelines as we continue to acquire more tools. We must look beyond the individual tools and the "clutter" they create. In addition, we must do this in a way that allows us to accommodate the required tools, which create the necessary audit logs that we are mandated to collect, handle, and assimilate as required by the myriad audit and regulatory agencies overseeing our enterprises and industry.

As part of this usage strategy, not only must we assess our individual environment, but also the expectations of the security practitioner and the impact on the bottom line. Later, we perform a cost–benefit analysis associated with this effort to help determine how much we can or should allocate to it, and what the "return" to the enterprise will be. This is especially important in today's "leaner" IT enterprise environments.

But first, let's return to our SETI analogy. As the technology evolved, the SETI scientists found that they (not the extraterrestrials) were able to collect and store all the radio waves that they had received. Now it became a matter of sifting through all this data to make some sense of it. Their ability to collect and store the data had overwhelmed their ability to analyze and filter the data. The solution they arrived at was to undertake a massive task of parallel computing, whereby the data would be distributed to systems for processing in their "unused time," under the form of a screen saver (see: http://www.seti.org).

As security practitioners, we face a similar dilemma: we have countless collectors (security event log generators) generating countless volumes of data. Yet given current resources, we don't have the necessary processing power or even procedural methodology to process or analyze the data to make intelligent use of it.

Similarly, today's security practitioners also deal with enormous amounts of information generated from the modern security toolsets alone. We maintain that it is all useful information serving some purpose, but when it comes down to it, we are left to wonder how much is actually available to process and use, or to reference when the need arises, or just to review on a regular basis. The reality of the matter is that even though we have the data, very little of it is easy for us to reference, let alone analyze or process in a simple manner, yet we spent countless thousands of dollars collecting and storing it, not to mention the practice of archiving it locally, or off site, purely for the ability to say we are doing so. But, truthfully, we must ask ourselves how useful is all this "information."

Going forward, we will need to solve the rest of this problem—we need to put this data to work for us in a practical sense, and in such a way that we start to see real benefits, both to us as security professionals and to the enterprises that we are employed to support. But first, it would be useful to address one obvious, underlying question, and that is, how did we actually get to this point of having more data then we can practically use or intelligently process?

It started with the first realization by the security practitioners that audit logs were necessary, well documented in the DoD *Evaluation Criteria for Trusted Computer Systems,* 1983. Early on, we had audit logs that merely wrote over themselves on a regular basis, somewhat like the airliner flight recorder with its looping data tape—the data was captured continuously but it had a short lifespan, as it was being constantly overwritten. At the time, the hope was that if the data was ever needed it could be recovered near the time it was available. Anything older than some preassigned value of minutes/hours/days was considered to be no longer necessary or of any value.

Amazingly, this approach was perfectly acceptable for quite some time in the field, and today there are still EDP systems that support this methodology with their audit logs. Having implemented a consolidated logging approach in the enterprise, I often find that I must collect logs from certain systems at specific times, as I have been told, "If you don't collect it by midnight, it'll be overwritten." So, despite the seemingly odd nature of this approach to collecting "valuable" audit data (by overwriting it on a regular basis), it is still considered disposable today. This practice should be considered a key driver for establishing a centralized, or systematic, approach to audit and trace log consolidation. It also highlights the critical need for the development of more sophisticated approaches to managing the data.

Also in need of review is the assignment of "value" on these audit logs. For many security practitioners, it is considered a dreaded but "required" component of any system, that one must always have an audit trail. However, few recognize the actual value of these logs until they are needed for some case analysis, event reconstruction, or other similar task that requires the "audit event data" to be available in a properly maintained and retrievable audit log. How many times during the height of a security "incident" have specific logs been requested or searched out, only to have them found to be overwritten, or not turned on and thus not to be in existence at all? Better yet, you find out that the very system that you request logs from had just been audited and it was known that it didn't produce the necessary logs, yet they were still not enabled. The system administrator was either slow in the process of getting the logs turned on, or was planning on just filing for a waiver from compliance, never with the intent of enabling the logs due to resource or technology shortages.

So, it is quite evident that audit logs must exist (even if they won't after midnight tonight). For the purposes of this discussion, we focus primarily on security audit logs, and touch on some related logs, as there are growing numbers of logs from all types of systems that are now available. In addition, it is important to maintain the focus of our objective from the perspective of security practitioners, as we are here to secure the enterprise and to use all relevant tools at our disposal to perform this function without burying ourselves under megabytes of useless data. But, as I point out in the chapter on correlation, it can sometimes be advantageous to insert additional system logs that go beyond logical security audit logs. One example of this might be physical security logs, which can track the coming and going of system users, which, in turn, might be correlated with network log-ons to ensure that on-site log-ons are accompanied by the physical presence of the account holder. But we save this type of correlation, and take it further, at a later point in this writing.

Another driver, or answer to the question of how did we get to this point of distributed data overload, is the proliferation of security tools and the corresponding increase in the output of logs or reports. There has been a noticeable industry trend toward specialized security tools in response to the growing need for security, both at the enterprise level as well as at the system level.

In the early days of network security, there were usually host logs of log-on activity, and maybe logs from the border router that held the ACLs (access control lists) that acted as the enterprise firewall (remember those early Cisco routers and the arguments with the network folks about the need for these ACLs?). Later, as the first enterprise firewalls appeared on the scene, they naturally included some degree, or minor form, of audit logging. However, these were nothing more than a low-level form of activity logs, all rolled into a single flat file, often using the old standard "roll-over" methodology, so that only a short time-period of logs was held locally. Initially, they were probably not even collected or viewed in their raw form, despite the fact that the device had been configured to perform this logging. The point is that today, as then, logs may be created, but oftentimes they are neither utilized, nor readily available, and as such are nothing more than a burden to the system. But, from the auditors' perspective, they were a required component of the system if only for the ability it gave them to say, "Yes, we have audit logs." Today, however, the auditors are beginning to ask a few more questions, and there is a real need to prove that the logs exist and are readily viewable or accessible. It is not even unusual anymore for them to be requested on random dates, for which there must be valid, auditable event records.

So, as mentioned previously, as systems evolved beyond the enterprise's perimeter firewall, there began a proliferation of tools. Soon after this, additional security tools arrived on the scene. For example, with respect to just firewalls, at one point, I personally counted 36 different vendors. One vendor went so far as to call itself, "Firewalls R Us." (But they were not long for this world, presumably due to copyright laws.)

One leader in the proliferation of security tools was intrusion detection systems (IDSs), which served us up with both host-based IDSs and network-based IDSs. Next came the network traffic security analysis tool, the host file integrity monitor, the enterprise security policy monitor, even the Honeypot, and then enter the "authentication server" market.

Although it is not exactly a system security tool, authentication is a key component of any enterprise security architecture. While host authentication has taken a backseat in the enterprise environment for authentication, network authentication servers have taken hold.

For remote access, RADIUS (Remote Dial-In User Service) servers became the norm for VPN (virtual private network) or RAS (remote access servers), which were originally dial-up, and then as infrastructures became segmented, authentication between "zones" emerged. These acted as gates between different intranet zones, normally in the form of "strong authentication," or two-factor authentication. System administrators were required to authenticate with a stronger mechanism for their system administrative access even within the network. This became more acceptable as the enterprise finally began to recognize the 80/20 rule for risks: 80 percent of the threats were internal, whereas only 20 percent were external. As a result, today there exist these bastions of authentication in the form of servers, all acting as key "gates" in the enterprise, but varied in their function, and whom or what they serve. Not surprisingly, these gates also represent more key components that must be monitored, and will undoubtedly create even more audit logs, and important ones at that. (At this point in time, you should be asking yourself, just how many authentication servers do I have in my enterprise today, and what is happening

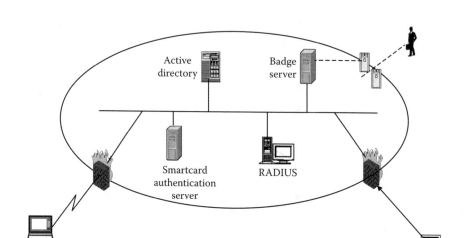

**Figure 1.1 Authentication server environment**

to all these logs?) To illustrate this point, Figure 1.1 depicts an enterprise security architecture and displays just a few of the common authentication servers, and to whom or what they may provide service. It is hoped that this underscores the need to recognize and to consider including them in your consolidation strategy. The ability to correlate system activity with authenticated users can provide very high value not only during the course of an investigation, but also in establishing regular rules of access to the network infrastructure.

At this point, one may begin to wonder about the grand scheme of audit log consolidation and correlation, and how the authentication server fits into the picture. For a moment though, let's return to the example of including physical building access logs in your correlation suite. Say, for example, you were to attempt to correlate your domain log-on with building/badge access records to ensure that the physical carbon-based unit (i.e., human user) was physically present to log on to the domain. In so doing, you just might overlook the RAS component. Now, let's say you enter your RAS or VPN authentication server, which, it is hoped, consists of some form of two-factor authentication mechanism that may or may not be a single image (with a possible backup, but still has one logical image). Let's assume you want to ensure that the appropriate user logging on to the internal domain has validly accessed the network, either by walking onto the property and having his badge scanned by a reader, or has remotely accessed the system through an authorized dial-up RAS or VPN system.

**Table 1.1 Sample Correlation of Physical/Logical Access to Domain Access**

| Date Stamp | Time | User | Source | Action | Alert Status |
|---|---|---|---|---|---|
| 3/1/04 | 7:30 | Psmith | Badge Svr | Access | None |
| 3/1/04 | 7:44 | Psmith | Active Directory | Access | None |
| 3/1/04 | 7:32 | tjohnson | Badge Svr | Access | None |
| 3/1/04 | 7:58 | tjohnson | Active Directory | Access | None |
| 3/1/04 | 8:01 | sjones | RADIUS Svr-VPN | Access | None |
| 3/1/04 | 8:03 | sjones | Active Directory | Access | None |
| 3/1/04 | 8:05 | thackel | Active Directory | Access | FLAG |

To verify that this is what in fact has happened, you would have to collect all the authorized RAS authentication system logs as well as the building reader's badge-in logs, which should have a direct correlation to every user by some common key or extension to a common identifier (each user with a log-on ID should have a physical badge identifier). Next, you would have to perform an "after the fact" correlation to determine a one-to-one match of physical or logical access to each user. In instances of mismatch (i.e., a system log-on, without the physical presence of the user or a recognized RAS session; see the final account record for "thackel" in Table 1.1. It has been noted as just such a case and thus comes across as a *Flagged* event), it is possible that you have detected a shared account access, an unauthorized modem pool, or VPN gateway, or, in the worst-case scenario, an unauthorized network gateway. This is not beyond belief, given the ease with which a network gateway can be set up in today's world. In this example, the security team would only get an alert in the case of a mismatch; not all the accesses that occurred in this example, only the flagged events, would be reported.

Table 1.1 illustrates the myriad systems that could be incorporated into your security audit log consolidation and correlation. This also demonstrates how the proliferation of these components has become both a burden and potentially a benefit if they were put to proper use. In the previous example, the systems highlighted generate thousands of records a day, rarely looked at or used, except in particular cases of investigation. But through the establishment of a regular working review (automated in this case) that then mines the data through correlation and produces relevant output, you have now added value to this once stagnant data.

With Table 1.1 in mind, let's continue to entertain the question of how we got here. The simple answer is that we got "here" as a result of the evolution of the EDP environment. As tools and functions blossomed (and bore fruit), each subsequent generation of systems added more logs, logs, and more logs (to the fire known as enterprise security)! Oftentimes, the sole reason for the generation of a log was simply, "Because audit said so." Occasionally, the management of a system called for the generation of a log, especially in the case of an authentication system, as nearly all of them required some form of troubleshooting at one time or another. This typically involved the reviewing of the logs to see what had happened. In this case, this led these particular logs to be kept in a more manageable form, which actually rendered them (heaven forbid) accessible. You may find in your own exploration (and counting) of your enterprise's authentication servers that there are a surprising number of logs not in the overwrite stage, as this is one area where they have actually been recognized as having added some value. Of course, this will not be the case in all instances. For example, I have personally seen some environments where if there is a problem with the ID on the authentication server, another ID is simply created to avoid the expense of investigating the reason or source of the problem.

At this point, we can now see at a very high level what may exist as a result of vast amounts of data, generated from a wide variety of systems, hosts, and tools—all with valid reasons for their existence. And, once these entities have been validated, they then require some form of audit logging. We're all familiar with these types of systems. Maybe we have even done our best to ensure that each performs at its required level of logging.

But, how useful are these logs? And, what value should be applied to them? And, how much more value can be added when they are correlated either on a one-to-one basis or in category groups? This is where our journey begins. Many questions remain: what to do with all this data? Should we even bother? Is there a cost-benefit ratio that can be established? And, most important, how do we justify this endeavor beyond the security arena, i.e., at the enterprise level?

To answer the first question, how useful are these logs, we must ask further questions: What are our requirements? Are we meeting them today? Chapter 2 delves into the who, what, and why questions that need to be asked, and some sample scenarios.

What I find amazing, in my experience, is what surfaces when you begin to ask the question around the security environment, "What exists out there currently," particularly, if you have just announced that you have a strategy to improve the situation with respect to audit logs. Many more answers appear than you had originally thought possible. Every security practitioner who has been through an audit realizes that an audit is required to ensure that everyone is keeping the appropriate levels of records. But, as previously pointed out, this is mostly so that they can answer, "Yes, we have logs." But, knowing that their hearts are not in it, these logs are typically much less sufficient than what is actually needed to serve a valid purpose. Yet, more times than not, time, dollars, and resources are not in adequate supply to even consider doing it right, so it lands on one of those all-too-familiar lists of "when I have time."

Once you have decided to embark on the audit log consolidation journey, you need to enter into what I call the discovery phase of the project. This can be quite an eye-opener, in terms of how many various system managers will come forward with their audit log needs once they hear that someone has initiated just such a project. Not surprising is how they will be more than happy to turn over their audit responsibilities to a central organization. (Now you are probably saying, "Of course, they are going to give it you. Who doesn't want to give away some tasks?") But, the point is that they usually are not just saying, "Here it is," but are asking "How do you want it," or "How can I give it to you so that it is a useful part of your project, and let me know when you want to begin testing and when can you put it into production?"

Their motivation is, we hope, twofold: it is somewhat due to the fact they want to relinquish a task. But, in addition, it is to address that lingering knowledge that the audit logs need to be done better. And, with that knowledge is the hope that a focused effort will indeed make the whole process more valuable to the enterprise. However, keep in mind that you may encounter unwilling parties as you begin your investigation of potential candidate logs for consolidation and correlation. You may find groups that are wholly unwilling to grant you access to their domain. Or, they may not be willing to give up information on their systems through the release of their logs for one reason or another. In some cases, this is simply due to the fact that they just don't have them, although they know that they should, but are not willing to admit it. Or, it can be a case of fear in the sense that it is going to be one more "enterprise" task or project that they don't have the time to participate in, and it will become one more burdensome task on their overworked system.

No matter the reasons, you will likely find sectors of resistance, so it is important that your project show some form of clear benefit to the systems directly, and be of minimal impact to the systems involved. In addition, it should demonstrate an overall benefit to the enterprise. We talk more about this in Chapter 8, once we have determined the strategy and approach, and have rationalized the project (if only to ourselves initially). Then, we walk through how to "take it on the road."

As part of your strategy development, a decision must be made as to which objective of consolidation this project is intended to address. There are a couple of distinct log consolidation objective paths, or approaches, you may decide to follow.

The first approach is purely to serve the purposes of audit log consolidation for security analysis and event correlation for a set amount of time back in history. This option is solely related to security; its goal is to make better use of the existing logs being generated by the diversity of systems and security event generators throughout your enterprise. This methodology has multiple benefits. First, it can give you a better view of your enterprise from a security perspective. Second, it can potentially provide advanced views through the correlation of the various devices across your environment, as we have begun to illustrate here. And third, it can possibly show you threats, vulnerability, or actual coordinated attacks that may be occurring, which would ordinarily not be evident by viewing the logs independently (we give some further examples of these types of events in Chapter 7, under one of the case analysis studies). In my view, this approach is the most valuable to the enterprise. The ability to gain further intelligent output from data you are already collecting I see as a high-value addition to your enterprise security architecture. The market shares this view, with the development of multiple COTS (commercial off-the-shelf software) products. These are products that provide such capabilities, although their approaches differ within this correlation category (and we talk about this when we discuss forming your evaluation criteria for COTS product selection in this area in Chapter 8).

The second approach, or methodology, to security audit log consolidation contains the entire first objective, and, in addition, attempts to provide for an additional benefit to the enterprise as well as the system that is supplying the log data by providing in-depth forensics capabilities through archival. In this case, the consolidation effort collects all of the security-relevant data, and in its complete form, not just the basis event data. All the security-relevant data is tagged so that each record clearly identifies its original system. Then the centralized system performs the security correlation in the same manner as the first approach, but now it also has the added responsibility of preserving the record and eventually moving it to an archive in compliance with your enterprise audit log record retention requirements. This added function (performing the collection and the retention) can be a selling point to the system administrators from whom you are asking for the logs, and can also provide a higher degree of assurance that the logs are actually being retained as per the retention policy of your enterprise.

Of course, this second approach comes at a much higher cost for the processing and retention/archival, but depending on the enterprise, its methodology of billing—even within the organization in some cases—can be recovered via internal "billing pools." Or, if the organization has been audited (by their internal audit organization or an external audit agency), with specific findings related to audit log retention noncompliance issues, then that can also motivate the funding machine to support your centralized approach as it would put them back into compliance. It is obvious that this second approach could be much more costly and complex, and add much more responsibility to the security team that is initiating the consolidation project. However, through an in-depth, cost-benefit analysis, and review of past security issues, you may be able to justify adopting the second approach for the good of the overall enterprise. We talk more about each of these two approaches in Chapters 5 and 6.

My personal experience consists of security event reviews, correlation, and collection across the enterprise for over 15 years (the first 10 years through custom-developed applications, thanks to the availability of UC Davis interns local to our site—thanks Andy) and collections of logs from a limited number of security event generating systems, the first being in the dial-up arena through the combining of the dial-up access servers, authentication server, and the host log-on records.

By combining these audit logs, I could see who was coming through the RAS devices, and then which IDs were logging on to the enterprise host systems (mainframes at the time, running ACF2). By doing this I should have recorded a match between each RAS session and a coinciding mainframe session. (Recognize that there will be some natural mismatch if the user decided after accessing the system that she didn't really want to start a session and had merely logged off.) But, for the "average" session, there was a record of a RAS access session with a valid two-factor authentication, attributable to an individual account holder, followed by an initiated/completed host mainframe access session under a matching host mainframe individual account. Because there was no natural internal communication between these systems, it was possible for a combination of different accounts to be used across one logical session which could indicate sharing of accounts. (It is possible that an authorized RAS user might have enabled a remote session and then turned the session over to another mainframe user who was not authorized for remote access, either as friendly sharing, or via a stolen account.)

Other mismatched scenarios might have indicated unreported lost RAS accounts, when there was a valid RAS session but no valid host mainframe account, which resulted in a form of a mismatch, and thus a security flag was raised. There would be one or more records of the valid RAS access, but no resulting valid host access. The correlation would flag the RAS access, as lacking a host access, indicating the user opened a RAS session but initiated no further valid access. In these cases, we soon found that there was an inordinate amount of invalid host access attempts, so we then began to correlate security error records to further prove our theory of mismatches.

The first approach, as you can see, can be of great use but does require a specific methodology and defined rule set, which can result in valid flagged security events; some may be obvious and programmed in, and others may only become more apparent once the data is correlated and analysis results show some security event value.

The second approach being broader in scale for compliance through clearly established procedures for audit log collection and retention in order to comply with established corporate policies, shows a clear benefit to the enterprise.

These are just two examples of two high-level objectives that can be pursued when embarking on your enterprise audit log consolidation and correlation project; one focused solely on the security aspect, i.e., strengthening your security program and posture; and the second can accomplish that plus ensure audit log retention compliance as well, and possibly benefit the security aspect by having much more data within reach of the security organization during in-depth case studies or forensics sessions. Hopefully by reviewing the proposals and what is involved in each of these methodologies/objectives, you will be able to make the best decision going forward, that proves to be both achievable as well as valuable to your enterprise.

To assist you in making this decision as to which approach to employ, the case study and analysis section show the potential benefits of either approach, and depending on the availability of resources, show clear benefits that are in line with your corporate goals and objectives. In many cases, as we have worked through this consolidation effort in multiple environments, other added benefits have emerged that we didn't see when initiating the project, but became readily apparent when all the data was in one place, and the appropriate tools were available to manipulate the data, or external requests came in to the team who had control over the consolidated repository of data.

It is my hope that through your review you will experience not only the benefits identified herein, but also the unexpected benefits unique to your enterprise that you will only find by beginning some execution in whole or a portion of the methodologies described. Even if a small implementation is initiated, I strongly believe benefits can be had, both the known and the unknown benefits, as each implementation has experienced this based on past history.

Say, for example, that just the RAS environment, as described previously, is to be addressed. This is a high-risk area and not growing as much today, with the emergence of VPNs and wireless (don't even get me started here; I'm now rolling in access point logs, the additional authentication servers, and whatever else I can get my hands on in this area, as we all know its explosive growth sees no bounds going forward). The point being even selecting one "like" environment of security event logging devices and consolidating and correlating them, should be able to have a clear benefit to you, the security professional, responsible for protecting the enterprise, and if the second methodology is chosen, the benefit may extend to the system owners/administrators from whom the logs are collected.

So, with all this said, and the overview of the potential gains through the various approaches depicted (or variations of them), it is hoped that this book will provide you with the tools, descriptions, and methods to benefit from this approach and the experiences gained over the past 10 years worth of work in this area of enterprise information security.

For the seasoned information security professional, there should be immediate potential benefits to reviewing each of these approaches. For the novice just entering the field, the definitions of systems, and what events they record or log become apparent. Then, the described correlations are a fast-forward introduction to security log event analysis, which should bring you up to date on this fairly recent methodology as it is now being sold through a multitude of products, and this writing should assist you in selecting the appropriate level for your enterprise.

## Chapter 2

# The "Why" of Consolidated Audit Logging

We have to dig deeper in the "why" of auditing and logging. We have outlined the need for it at a very high level, and know from "best practices" that it is a requirement in any EDP environment, but can you today in one sentence answer the question, "Why do we do audit logging?" Everyone today in an EDP position has oversight groups, committees, or industry-specific organizations, all of which have rules and regulations as to how the business is run, what models work for them, and what degrees of "compliance" are required. In this section we try to evaluate at a high level what these requirements are, why they are drivers to what we are trying to accomplish in the form of audit logging, and how this consolidation approach can help you to both meet these requirements and provide a value to the business.

We all know that we have to do auditing and we go about it blindly or think that we are doing it, but now we have to go back a step and figure out the why and then possibly better formulate an enhanced approach to meet this need. Hopefully the end result of this analysis will result in us actually effectively and efficiently performing the required audit logging so that it is more than checking off an audit task list and we make it more of a usable function. In addition, when performing the analysis in preparation for evaluating our audit needs, we will have a much better understanding of what is being done today within our infrastructure.

In looking at requirements, if you are a financial institution or a healthcare institution, then you are already under high scrutiny in respect to tracking records of your activities and transactions, which must be recorded in some form of logging mechanism by mandate or regulation. Regarding this issue, what do we do? Do you know against what specific requirement you are logging? Now is the time to begin researching that to ensure you know what your target objective is for your logging. This may even require an external assessment or reference from your compliance office to determine not only what your internal policy states (you do have an internal corporate enterprise security policy) or you may even get directed to an external industry mandate (or even government mandate as mentioned further on). Whatever the resource, mandate, or directive you find, it must be matched against what you are doing now, or plan to do once you initiate the enhancements to your audit logging program.

Based on this preliminary research you then need to look at how it really relates to your arena and if it specifically applies, there is nothing worse than doing more than you are supposed to be doing (not that we really run a chance of exceeding audit log requirements, but it could happen).

So let's look at some of the reasons we are doing all this auditing; it has to be for more then just satisfying the never-ending audits as mentioned previously which are there for a purpose and actually are more than just keeping us in a job (closing audit findings). There are actual benefits from having a fully functional and coordinated internal audit logging program/infrastructure.

From a pure "auditing" standpoint, the basis of any security program is the ability to "monitor" the system, access, or events within an EDP system or environment. Referencing a few sources can provide additional definition in this space, to help us determine what we should be achieving with our enhanced audit logging system. In its purest form, the *Webster's New World Dictionary* defines audit as "the formal checking of financial records." We merely want to mimic this definition, highlighting the "checking" aspect of the "records," which in our case are those generated by our security or security-related systems. Pulling from an internationally recognized standard, the British Security Standards BS17799 has specific statements toward "Accountability." Although not in the top four requirements of this security standard, the fifth and very notable criterion is that for "accountability," which speaks to the responsibility of the organization to be able to establish and show accountability. This by definition requires that there be a record of actions, which is the genesis of this whole logging ordeal. In fact, the responsibility of accountability has been a caveat/

centerpoint of security for over 20 years. The Trusted System Evaluation Criteria from the U.S. Department of Defense clearly defines accountability and its relation to logging and auditing as:

> Requirement 4—ACCOUNTABILITY—Audit information must be selectively kept and protected so that actions affecting security can be traced to the responsible party. A trusted system must be able to record the occurrences of security-relevant events in an audit log. The capability to select the audit events to be recorded is necessary to minimize the expense of auditing and to allow efficient analysis.

This 20-year-old passage calls out the needs for auditing and logging as well as "why" it must be put into place and the "what": for the capture of "security-relevant events." It even cites drivers of today, specifically cost, clearly calling for the need to "minimize the expense of auditing."

The more current BS17799 doesn't even go into this depth of explanation, but merely mandates the need for accountability or necessarily who is to be held accountable. So when it comes to the security practitioner's responsibility, we are left to our own devices to meet the requirement. The first and most obvious choice is to rely on the resources built into the systems—the audit logging tools—which come inherently in nearly all systems and applications. So we blindly mandate that audit logging be enabled in order to meet the enterprise requirements for accountability. Here is one key driver for establishing a manageable logging system/server for the enterprise, which is to have the ability to meet such an accountability standard. Even though it is of course "best practice," it may also be a mandate within your industry as long as it does not disrupt your business practices or put undo burden on your IT resources.

Another directive can come from localized regulatory policy or practices, such as in California SB1386, where it is required to follow specific notification of data owners of any record of a "breach of security." Because this notification requirement can be very encompassing (and costly), it is imperative that accurate records be kept of any suspect breaches and ability to defend against when an actual breach has occurred, or ability to prove that such a breach didn't occur. This requirement now starts defining what you should be logging and monitoring, incidents or transactions that may provide some indication of a breach. We talk more on the "what" to log in Chapter 4, but it can be tied back to the basics of "what are the requirements." In this case it is to prove or disprove that a breach may have occurred. Although a relatively new law (California SB1386), for California businesses it still must be prepared for in the case of a breach or ability to detect one and furthermore defending why your firm should not have to make consumer notifications if no suspected breach has occurred (and the corresponding cost savings of not having to perform the notifications).

And for those firms outside California, they should also be preparing for similar laws in their jurisdictions, as many jurisdictions are looking to the California law as a strong consumer protection mechanism, and many states are considering passing similar legislation as well as a possible federal version of similar legislation. Only by having the appropriate mechanisms and tools to identify a breach will an enterprise be able to comply with the law and defend against why they were not required to make customer notifications of possible losses of data, as they had records showing that no such breach could have occurred.

In an interesting twist on security in respect to the "why" of logging and accountability, there have been some circles of discussion that have the audacity to suggest possibly it would be better to not be so extensive in our logging, monitoring, and auditing, so that fewer suspected breaches would be detected and thus would result in less likelihood of having to make the consumer/user notifications if a system breach occurred. (I call this the ostrich approach to auditing: putting your head in the cyber hole in the sand.) This type of approach would possibly conceal the case of potential personal information being revealed (which would be cause for the user notifications mentioned earlier). Of course this should not be the course of action in any professional and ethical organization, so the diligent logging route must be taken in a coordinated and cost-effective manner to best serve the business. So indirectly the logging requirement must be met for the enterprise to meet its legal obligations at a much higher level.

Following on this line of the need to keep audit logs in order to be able to identify the fact of a beach occurring or not occurring further defines your logging requirements. If your log consolidation initiative is to be used for this purpose, this says that you are maintaining it for the purpose of computer forensics for investigative analysis. This now defines that your logging initiative will be more extensive in both the amounts of data to be collected and the sources from which you gain this data. We cover more of this in Chapter 4, but for now let's go with the fact that this driver (computer or investigative forensics based on possible legal defense) is a strong driver for the program and should be used in your business case to gain support for your initiative.

Aside from the overarching government and industry standards, we mentioned the existence of your own corporate policy. We hope there is one, and that in it there is such a mandate for audit logging of "key or critical devices." This is best practices and common sense from a security perspective. In analyzing this driver, however, we may find that although it has been in existence for years, and the systems we manage in our

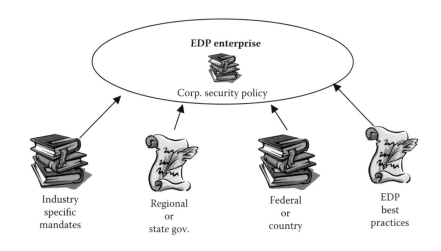

**Figure 2.1   Regulatory factors influencing auditing decisions**

enterprise are functionally capable of generating logs (in some cases even "overgenerating" logs), what is actually the probability that your "critical systems" are even configured to generate the logs? And that they are supported in an effective manner and there is the ability to review these logs in an intelligent manner. A quick sampling or review of their status in respect to logging will answer this question.

It is quite obvious that there is a wide variety of regulatory drivers to perform audit logging in an accurate, useful, and effective fashion. These regulatory drivers come from within your enterprise, nearby your enterprise (i.e., industry-led standards), regional or statewide drivers, and potentially countywide drivers. Figure 2.1 illustrates a very high level of some of these drivers and how we need to recognize them and attempt to adhere to them if we can find and identify those that apply to our enterprise.

We did mention the possibility of hiring an independent third party to conduct our survey of our current state in relation to audit logging, and one would hope if you have the correct subject matter expert on this analysis team, she would be able to assist in identifying all the regulations that would apply to your enterprise.

Last, there is the question of whether these "critical system" logs are preserved in a recoverable fashion for the required log retention period (commonly 60 to 90 days at a minimum). The point here is that if you don't feel that you are in complete compliance across the board, this may be a key motivator/driver to establish your centralized log consolidation methodology, as it will be establishing compliance versus replacing an existing practice. As a result of a survey of your current status in respect to logging, it shouldn't be surprising that your overburdened system administrators of critical devices may not be meeting this audit logging mandate to the letter of the policy.

This aspect of relying on system managers of distributed critical devices for maintaining their own audit logs to the level of your corporate policy also brings up another key issue. What does it take for you, the security manager, to conduct a forensics investigation under a distributed audit logging architecture? As an example, if an "issue" (the politically correct word these days to describe a security incident; we no longer have "incidents"; we now have "issues") were to occur on one of your distributed systems, obviously that will be the first log to be pulled and analyzed, assuming it exists for some period of time after the incident. The author has seen systems that have a variety of audit log configurations, some set so high that the volume of logging data is so large it ends up overwriting itself once every 12 hours, or the audit logging level is set so low, what data or records that are captured are of little or no use (System Up, System Shutting Down). And finally in some cases the logging is found just to be set on a regular overwrite period ranging from once every 24 hours to once a week, in which case any detection of an incident greater than five to seven days would have no forensic data available to go back to analyze. So returning to the example of having to perform an investigation using distributed logging mechanisms, here are some of the hurdles with which the security manager and his investigation team will have to deal.

In the hypothetical case of an internal corrupt Web server (a popular and often easy target), the first logs pulled will be the Web server logs. As the security manager you probably don't have that server administrator on your team, therefore, a request has to be made to pull these logs for the time period in question, and sent in a readable format to you, the investigative team. Then the questions come up whether it was suspected to be a direct attack by personnel, or a code attack. If it was suspected to be a personnel attack, then the local log-on records must be pulled, and in some cases where the server sits in a protected zone, there are gateway logs, or authentication logs to be pulled (remember this from our initial discussion; they come up more and more, as we become more reliant on access logs in general), and they are probably managed by yet a different IT person or group. And if the attack is suspected to be code related, then the enterprise virus server may need to be interrogated to determine which machines it had distributed patches to as well as if it keeps logs of hosts from which it has recently eradicated a virus (this is actually a loggable event in many enterprise virus applications; they receive reports from enterprise virus clients when they detect and eradicate a virus).

Again, this device (the enterprise virus server) is probably under yet another administrator (usually someone in server support or client desktop support), and thus an arrangement must be made to obtain a copy of the past few days of reports from this server or group of servers, recognizing they too may have a distributed architecture for maintaining a high confidence of virus control. Again, it quickly becomes apparent how this may be a driver for your consolidated logging approach, because under this same event, in a distributed logging architecture, if useful logs exist at each of these endpoints, the effort of obtaining the respective logs in a readable format can be time consuming and resource intensive. Then comes the task of actually performing the analysis. The capture or collection of these logs can take a day or two and that is even before any analysis can be performed.

Now that your investigative team has collected all these various logs, the task of filtering through them becomes daunting. Normally it is purely a manual method, hoping that they can be read through some common method, and sorted by time stamp, or possibly by device or error number, recognizing they probably won't have much in the form of common denominators in their native format. The ideal situation would be to already know what fields are in each log, already have some form of common denominator beyond just time stamp (and even that may not be common, as many systems are subject to time shifts and thus their log times are different, and, therefore, even time stamps cannot be relied upon as a good or acceptable common denominator). Thus if all conditions are in your favor, an investigation can be conducted even under a distributed logging architecture, although the odds of this happening (all conditions being met) will vary depending on your environment. It's time to conduct an investigation in this scenario, look at your environment, and determine what degree of confidence you have that this can be done.

In this example, the pitfalls of a distributed logging approach start to become obvious, but to further put it into perspective, we have assembled a quick "time to analysis" matrix which provides a rough calculation of the elapsed time it would take to conduct such an investigation under this type of distributed logging methodology over three servers; this matrix is illustrated by example in Table 2.1.

In this example, the chart assumes there are three distributed systems that have logs which must be reviewed as part of this investigation. In the left column are the variables that come into play when manually collecting logs from distributed input sources. The "Access to Log" variables take into account whether the system administrator is close at hand, say, directly reporting into your Information Security Office (ISO), in which case, it is not more than 0.5 of a day at most to get the log. This system administrator is most likely in another group, but, hopefully, still stationed

**Table 2.1  Time to Analysis Matrix**

| Time to Investigate under a Distributed Logging Architecture | Workdays to Recovery Log | Distributed System 1 | Distributed System 2 | Distributed System 3 | Days to Recovery and Analysis |
|---|---|---|---|---|---|
| **Access to Log** | | | | | |
| System administrator is ISO Team | 0.5 | X | | | 0.5 |
| System administrator is on site | 1 | | X | | 1 |
| System administrator is remote | 2 | | | X | 2 |
| **Log Format** | | | | | |
| Logs have been previously captured, format | 0.5 | X | | | 0.5 |
| Logs never previously captured, unknown format | 2 | | X | | 2 |
| Logs unrecoverable | 0 | | | X | |
| **Analysis Method** | | | | | |
| Purely manual | 1.5 | | | | |
| Partial electronic search | 0.75 | | X | | 0.75 |
| Wholly electronically correlated | 0.5 | X | | | 0.5 |

on site and reachable in one business day, although if he is outside your group and at some remote location, it can easily be two business days to obtain the log and possibly more when time zone differences come into play.

The next area of conditionals comes in the format of the log in question. Under "Log Format," if the log has been previously obtained, so the format is known and readable, then it is a fairly reasonable consideration that you will be able to easily read and analyze it when you receive it this time around. Although if you have never received this log and are unaware what format it's coming to you in, then there is considerably more time spent on just getting it into a readable format. And finally there is the possibility that once you found the system administrator and inquired about the audit logs, you may find that the log was one of those "once an hour overwrites," and thus the log format is of little concern (because there is no log) and thus won't add any time to your format issue.

Finally, there is the ultimate analysis question: how are you going to analyze what you have finally obtained. If the log comes in a somewhat readable format, but not electronic, then the purely manual analysis method will take at least 1.5 days, with a dedicated resource (considering a single day's activity log from a minimal host can be 20,000 lines or longer). If there is some form of electronic medium to search the log, of course the timeframe is reduced, and under the best conditions the logs can be put into some form or a wholly electronic system for correlation. Then of course the task time is considerably shorter. And there are multiple electronic analysis methods, from a simple grep of the file individually, thus with no correlation between files, but at least an electronic search can be made of each file. Or there could be a methodology set up that allows you to put all the files into a single repository and then possibly do some form of correlation between the various files and devices, but this would rely on the ability to "normalize" these files such that they would be in a standard format. Unless you have set this up in advance, most forensics teams don't have the time or resources to do this for each investigation, and thus a combined correlated electronic analysis is normally not available when all the logs are distributed and only pulled together during the course of individual investigations.

It soon becomes obvious the log collection and times to execute can become greatly extended in a distributed audit logging method, and the above example only addresses the mostly technical aspects of the log collection. It doesn't even begin to take into the account the potential political barriers (nor can it). For example, what if one of the distributed systems is a gateway firewall managed by another division or unit of your firm, or worse yet, by one of your service providers for your long-haul lines, and they may be reluctant to even release "their" logs over "your" system, so the time to get over this hurdle cannot even be estimated and may drive the system to a "no log recoverable" category (which, of course, reduces your analysis time, but possibly further cripples your investigation due to the lack of data). Additionally, this example only indicates three distributed systems; in larger enterprises or "incidents," there could be a far greater number of systems, all subject to the time conditions along the left column. This type of estimate could be benchmarked against past investigations and the time-to-analysis figures could be updated to more accurately reflect your environment, either through increases in the values or possibly decreases due to a more structured and cooperative environment (unfortunately, possibly the exception rather then the rule in today's larger enterprises). And on a final note, these calculations are based on serial estimates to completion, as it can be fairly easily determined that you must first gain access to the log, then determine format and compatibility of it, and only then can you perform the analysis; so it's clear this is a serial process.

This scenario further points out the potential value of developing a consolidated approach to logging and auditing in your enterprise. The author and any experienced enterprise security manager know of the conditions stated in a distribution enterprise, and the hurdles of working within this framework. Thus we continue down the path of the "why" of security audit log consolidation building upon the forensics case study started here.

If computer forensics is one of your drivers for initiating your log consolidation project, a few items must be taken into account in your initial planning stages. Now is a good time to look at those or at least be aware of the differences beyond mere audit logging, as it may affect your decision process and possibly cost estimates, as you begin looking at the depth and complexity. To do it properly, logging for computer forensics brings in a whole different facet of information requirements because what you may be required to do for mere system audit requirements may not be to the depth that makes up good forensics. As we explore in Chapter 5, audit logging to best practices is actually sensible and may not call for the complete capture of all audit records, whereas for computer forensics, depending on the sensitivity of the system, or thoroughness of its logging, you may want to capture much more in the form of record content and logging information, as well as potentially longer retention periods, which may exceed the 60- to 90-day period cited earlier.

Examples of critical systems that can provide valuable information for forensics purposes of course would start with your firewalls, but now that we have logging servers for our virus detection and eradication, these may prove to be valuable sources of historical information, due to the fact many of today's attacks are virus based, and if your systems are correctly maintained (i.e., maintain current and dynamic updates, eradication, and reporting), then it can be a valuable resource in the forensics field. By possible correlating in-depth information of machines detected with a virus, and with any detected incidents either from your firewall, or possibly other internal devices (remember that corrupt Web server we spoke of?), then we might have a good path of data to be able to discover what actually happened. But this would rely on the fact that we did have all these records from these various devices and were able to cross-correlate them in an intelligent manner. This is all based on good record retention, from the appropriate sources, with the appropriate data.

In Chapter 5, we talk more of the detail of what to capture, but the point here on the "why" to do it becomes quite evident, and can even be traced back to that regulatory requirement having to report any potential issues or security breaches. And to further complicate matters, many forensics cases are not this easily defined; as new attack scenarios are emerging every day, it may not be as easy as tracking down an infected machine as a potential point of origin. More and more as we find new attack methodologies, we find we need new log data not previously identified, and thus need the full audit log, as we may not know what attribute field we will have to perform a search over for each future case. Therefore, computer forensics investigations require a high degree of detail and "drill down" to individual log fields that may not normally be considered critical, and thus under standard logging conditions, may not normally be captured.

Again the point here is that to really be able to ensure a successful logging program for forensics may require more extensive logging than currently conducted, or envisioned, so it is important to recognize the potential added costs and efforts. The author feels that the effort and costs are worthwhile given the value of the data when under an incident scenario in a large enterprise. Many times you find yourself in the proverbial mode of looking for the "needle in the haystack" scenario, but the larger the haystack in this case, the better, as you have that much more information to search which in this case can be a good thing. If you have the tools to conduct correlations and custom search them, that much more data isn't a bad thing, and it gives you the potential of making sense of something possibly not previously defined (as mentioned earlier with the newness of attacks now emerging). And from the author's perspective, nothing is more job satisfying in the course of an intense investigation than to be able to have the necessary data readily at your fingertips and be able to pull the proverbial "rabbit out of your hat" and produce relevant data, findings, or reports on the incident based on the your amassed security log record database.

And while we are on the benefits of why to do it via forensics, it warrants a short discussion on the tools that come into play when going into computer forensics or investigations utilizing system or security device audit logs. In nearly all cases, these systems that generate these very useful logs don't contain much in the way of reporting systems to dig into these logs, or they provide an export mechanism, but usually in only a very generic format and of course we can't seem to find the common threads among this log and those of another critical security system. So, if were are going to need a strong defensible forensics toolset, we cannot rely on distributed logs, on systems that may not have any form of reporting system to speak of, and furthermore based on logs from disparate systems that have little recognizable common threads to even begin forming the investigation around, necessary to build the "cyber" trail of events. So this just further justifies the "why" or motivation to being the evaluation of your systems, processes, and procedures to determine whether a log consolidation initiative is appropriate, cost-effective, and functionally required for your environment.

Turning to a standards body, in general you will find multiple emerging standards in the logging space, each with its own driver, but common in the recognition that logs contain valuable data; it is just a matter of being able to find the valuable data. To cite just one standard, NIST has been working a proposal for their FLUD approach (Framework for Logging Usability Data), which is attempting to establish a standard for logging usability metrics. This may be too specialized for our general enterprise security approach in the first cut, but the fact that such initiatives are underway shows the recognition of value in audit log data and the many uses that can be concocted, I mean, generated, from this data. Other logging standards are identified as we move forward, but our approach is not to go into the outer fringes of emerging or bleeding-edge technology but rather to utilize COTS (commercial off-the-shelf) products that are here today, and a viable alternative to leaving your logs distributed across your enterprise with minimal confidence levels that they are serving their purpose and are readily available during the course of a security investigation.

One of the standards of audit logging that can cause confusion is the plain old archiving of audit logs. In legacy systems, there are nightly backups of the server or production-level data from each application server. In some cases you will find that the system administrator has included in that nightly backup, the backup of system-level files as well, including the audit logs.

In some cases your centralized logging system may not be the optimal device to perform this function. Most systems on an enterprise level have the ability for nightly archiving of logs and data to a standard backup system. If the decision has been made to utilize your centralized log consolidation system as the forensic and investigative tool, but not the sole repository of the system logs, then the standard nightly backup system may still be utilized for this function. The differentiator between these two systems is that the one has the permanent (or at least archived version of your logs) and the centralized logging system that you are creating is utilized to satisfy the audit requirement of the system to be able to review the security events for security-related events and after-the-fact forensics investigations. These are two distinctly different functions, although both are requirements in most enterprise systems (the function of review and the ability to preserve activity on a host system or critical enterprise device). For the purpose of this exercise, we stay focused on the security aspects of security audit logging, and consolidation of these types of logs in support of the security objectives of the enterprise.

To touch on other motivating factors, when we look at log consolidation from a forensics perspective separate from the archival function as mentioned above and the regulatory compliance issues, we have a clear need to maintain complete records and a trail of what occurred (or at least within each individual device). The additional driver here is the correlation in support of the forensics and, as we saw, there are clear benefits from being able to correlate "like" data types, in an intelligent manner, with ease and little training.

# Chapter 3

# Taking Stock, What Is in Place Today

Before you can launch into a whole-scale revamping of your logging approach, you should perform an analysis of what you have in place today. This is important for several reasons: your consolidation approach should show efficient use of resources, cost consolidations (and possibly savings), and reduced forensics and investigative time; and, of course, better showing of audit ability that you can prove audit logs are retained, managed, and archived in a secure manner when your consolidation approach is laid out and executed appropriately.

Your evaluation of your current approach should target those audit log sources that you hope to eventually include in your log consolidation effort, both near-term and long-term goals. So, for instance, if you plan to start with key or critical firewall logs in phase one, and then expand to all firewalls and then farther out to authentication servers (password and strong authentication devices), network device logs, virus servers, and the like, then you should determine to what extent logging processes exist for each of these areas and are in place today. The broader you perform your initial survey, the higher the potential degree of savings and efficiencies you can realize from a consolidation effort over time, as well as forensics value (i.e., the ability to review these logs under an investigative situation) as we show when doing our case analysis of a consolidated enterprise implementation for logging.

**Table 3.1  Survey Questions**

| | |
|---|---|
| 1. | What forms of logging do you currently perform on this device? |
| 2. | What is the volume, amount of data, collected in one 24-hour period? |
| 3. | What is your retention period; that is, how long do you keep retrievable logs? |
| 4. | What are the formats for this retention? 30 days online, 30 days tape, 3 months CD? |
| 5. | What is the "write per second" timeframe? How many records per second are generated and logged? |
| 6. | Where are the logs stored today (locally on the box, locally on a nearby server)? |
| 7. | If stored externally, how are they transported to the external store (syslog, FTP, other)? |
| 8. | Is there a separate physical interface over which the logs are distributed out of the box? |
| 9. | What are the access control mechanisms over access to the stored logs? |
| 10. | Who reviews the logs? At what frequency? |
| 11. | What is the data classification of this log data (Company Secret, Confidential, Internal Use)? |
| 12. | Is there a log reporting system? How are the logs accessed and viewed? How many people in the organization are required to have access to these logs? |
| 13. | What are the nature of the reviews: are keywords searched, summaries, or just high-level eyeing of the log data? |
| 14. | Are there additional log review, storage, or analysis capabilities that you would like to have over this log data? If so, what are they? |

The logical first step is to take a survey of your current logging methodologies in the area that you first plan to address. If, for example, your first consolidations are to take place in your distributed firewall environment, then surveys of these target resources should be conducted. A sample survey questionnaire appears in Table 3.1. These questions are more from a process and procedural perspective, but most important for you, the technologist, designing and developing your consolidated logging approach based on these technical requirements.

Based on the answers from these surveys, and then matched to your policy or mandate that you are attempting to meet (as discussed in Chapter

2), you can then develop and draft a sample requirements matrix against which you will perform product selection if you are going down the path of the COTS (commercial off-the-shelf) approach. Or if, heaven forbid, you decide to develop your own log consolidation architecture, the results of this survey will be your driving requirements for your development effort (although given the wide array of COTS products in this area, this is not the recommendation of the author, unless you find your organization with such unique unsatisfied needs or requirements that none of the COTS vendors are able to meet, then maybe internally developed methodologies would be appropriate for your enterprise, but can come at a great cost. The author has done the "make versus buy" analysis on the first go-round and, due to the lack of viable COTS products in this space six years ago, discovered the software development costs associated with a "from scratch" development effort).

This survey must be completed for each data device targeted to feed your log consolidation effort. It obviously will be the requirements drivers now and in the future as you add to your enterprise log consolidation initiative. A quick run-through of the questions will further highlight the value of such a survey component.

## 1. What Forms or Levels of Logging Do You Currently Perform on This Device?

It is key to understand what they are doing today, and in what form. In many cases, only the lowest level of logging is enabled (or sometimes even none at all). If logging is enabled, you must find out to what degree; many devices, especially firewalls and network devices, have various levels of logging capability, which usually equates to a wide variance in volumes of data generated. The answer to this question may require extensive preparatory analysis of their current form of logging on that device. If they reply that logging is enabled but they are unaware of the "level" of logging, then you need to research the device and determine what the available logging levels are, as well as determine what level they are currently logging at this point. Then take a look at the logging records that are being captured, determine the relevancy of the log data, and whether they are capturing the appropriate level for your needs based on earlier requirement decisions (to meet minimum audit requirements, to satisfy governmental regulations, industry regulations, or your own internal computer forensics investigations).

This analysis can get in depth, as you may soon find that the logging level currently set does not match with your targeted requirements. If, for example, you are looking for minimum audit requirements, which may just require alert and access violation activity, with user identification where available, then a full high-level log setting that captures all device activity (allowed and disallowed) may be beyond your requirements and overburden your consolidation system with records exceeding your requirements. On the other hand, as is commonly found, the logging system is found to be at the lowest setting, indicating that only minimal information is being captured in this "system" or device log, and when analyzed, found to be of little use from an investigative or forensic standpoint. In this case, the next level up in the logging scale needs to be analyzed and determined as to whether it provides the level of detail you require for your investigative or forensic logging effort. Unfortunately sometimes the best way to perform this analysis is to turn the logging level up one notch, run it for a week, and then analyze the output to determine if the logging records captured at this level meet your needs.

It is recognized that the device documentation should provide you with this level of detail, but it is this author's experience that many times the product documentation does not accurately reflect or keep up with the level or revision of code on your devices, hence the need to look at actual output from the device over a period of time. At a minimum, the documentation can point you toward the appropriate level of logging, but may not contain all the fields or formats that appear at each level set in their logging scale. It soon becomes quite evident at this point how important each answer is to these survey questions, and how each can drive some degree requirements for your end analysis.

## 2. What Is the Volume, Amount of Data Collected in One 24-Hour Period?

This is an obvious, must know type of question, as it will drive the sizing of your centralized logging device based on volume metrics. You do have to recognize though that all these questions are interrelated, and each answer may or will affect the follow-on questions. Take, for example, Question 1 where we asked the nature of the logging currently being conducted. Potentially based on their answer and our follow-on analysis, we may find that their level of auditing is inadequate for our needs, or to meet policy requirements. But if in Question 2 they answer with some small volume of data, say 1 Mb a day, but our analysis indicates their logging should be set at a higher level, we'll have to re-estimate our sizing based on changes that we made when analyzing Question 1 in order to put their logging into audit compliance.

Other change factors that may affect their answer here in respect to volumes of data being collected is their retention schedule. If it is found that they are not in compliance with the audit log retention period, possibly retaining log records for too short a timeframe, and are also at the wrong level of logging (too low a setting), this could have an extensive impact on the volume of stored data that needs to be accounted for in your planning and design. For now, it's a matter of just collecting the answers, analyzing the data, re-estimating and answering the questions based on your analysis, and developing your requirements list for your product selection. We go through this whole sequence, but now just continue on the issues that emerge based on the survey questions.

## 3. What Is Your Retention Period; That Is, How Long Do You Keep Retrievable Logs?

This is an "if" question; i.e., "if" they perform logging in some manner, how long do they keep these logs in some recoverable format This is key, as an individual administrator's retention period usually varies from the corporate standard. You may find cases where they are in compliance because they have recently undergone a corporate audit, in which case they are either up to par, or under some form of "waiver from compliance." In this latter case, where they are out of compliance, it is often found to be a resource issue, either the box/system doesn't have enough horsepower to do its main function and do the necessary logging, or the storage is not available to keep the required amount of logs for the appropriate period of time. And in some cases, they just don't have the time to put the necessary logging into place with the appropriate level of analysis to determine what is correct. In this case, our effort/attention to logging can help them come into compliance or at least perform the analysis on what is necessary to bring them into compliance and also provide an "out of band" logging mechanism that won't overly affect their existing system and provide an off-the-box storage medium (your centralized logging system). This can be a win–win situation as you will now have a potentially very willing "customer" to work with for log consolidation and retention.

## 4. What Are the Formats for This Retention? 30 Days Online, 30 Days Tape, 3 Months CD?

Related of course to the previous question (what they are doing regarding logging and retention), the issue here is that you may find many different formats for log data retention, which may complicate matters if you absorb the collection of their logs and they still require access to them or the data contained within them.

The question somewhat leads to the answer in that it suggests methods we have seen in other distributed environments, as the age of the log grows and the volume, the longer the retention period, the more storage media are introduced. This is usually driven by the cost of the storage media, and even though these costs are dropping, cost is always an issue if there are tiers of lower cost methods. Online storage is of course more expensive than tape, which can be more expensive than plain old burned CD or jukeboxlike storage media; thus, where the logs are stored for longer periods of time, as a cost savings effort, the logs are migrated to lesser-cost storage media over time. For now, it's important to just capture this fact, and work it into your design, depending how "married" to this system the administrators are to the storage methodology for access to their aged logs. They may not care what the medium is, just as long as they continue to have access to the stored logs for the timeframe they are accustomed to in their legacy environment. In some cases, it is time to revamp the legacy storage medium, because the mere process of migrating the data between the various storage media may procedurally cost more than the perceived cost savings associated with the lower-cost storage medium.

## 5. What Is the "Write per Second" Timeframe? How Many Records per Second Are Generated and Logged?

This is an obvious key item in your design decision/product selection, as your system may be put to very high volumes when consolidating a wide variety of systems. Though in some cases, the end user/administrator may not have this level of detail, some simple analysis may have to be conducted to try to come up with some form of answer. It may be as simple as capturing the volume of raw data logged over a period of time and calculating the answer, which would be rudimentary at best, but at least gives some form of first estimate. Of course, this should be done over multiple periods of times and dates, as data inputs vary widely in network systems where high volumes of log records are being cut. The variables can be based on volumes of access (if it is a gateway system's logs or authentication system's logs), or it can also vary based on network location and bandwidth issues, where at certain times of day there are network-imposed latencies, and even though the end device may be generating logs at the same rate, the time to reach your network-based "collection" engine may be delayed due to network issues during particular times of the day or processing cycle. Also, the answer to this question has to be correlated to the next question on the location of their storage, whether it is done in real-time locally or remotely and for archival purposes whether it's done locally or remotely.

## 6. Where Are the Logs Stored Today (Locally on the Box, Locally on a Nearby Server, or Remotely)?

As mentioned previously, the answer to this question may affect some of the other answers given, such as logging times and retention methods. If they are doing logging at a local level (possibly on the very box generating the logs), you will most likely find low retention cycles, lowered levels of logging, and minimal reporting capabilities because they don't want to affect the processing power of the application server or network device itself. This can all be a good thing, because by introducing a centralized, managed logging methodology, you can be relieving their system of the logging burden, and actually providing a valuable service to them, and maybe even putting off their need for near-term box or device upgrades by relieving it of this service locally.

On the other side of the coin, you may find that the system administrator already has some form of "off-device" logging methodology established, which is a "best practice" from a security perspective. This best practice is usually put into place in order to have better control and protection of valuable system audit logs, knowing that they can be the second target of a system once it is compromised. Intelligent attackers will attempt to cover their tracks and will usually try to erase evidence of their entry into the system and subsequent data access or other covert activity they perform on the compromised host. So in response to this, the security-conscious administrator will sometimes off-load his logs to a separate server to thwart this type of action. (Usually only after it has happened to them, a system compromise, so if you find they are performing off-loading of their audit logs, don't follow up with the question, "So, when did your system get compromised?" That's just plain cruel.)

Your analysis of the answers to this question may come across as very helpful and beneficial to the system administrator if he is performing minimal or compliant logging on his local system, or may appear to be a duplication of an extensive effort he has already put into off-loading his logs to a separate server. If the latter is the case, you may have to perform some damage control, by promoting the benefits of a centralized logging system beyond mere off-loads of log data. You could potentially "sell" your service as method to free up their existing log server by returning it to their server pool for other uses, as you will now be collecting the logs in your centralized logging framework.

For now, just capturing and understanding what they are doing (and why) are the most critical points. You may find even extreme cases of off-loading logs, even to the point of wholly external entities to the enterprise such as in the case of a "managed security service," where the service is not run by your company but by a third party. In recent years there has been a growing trend to outsource various security services, and one of them has been logging, alerting, and monitoring systems by independent third parties, under the guise of cost savings through econ-omies of scale, and ability to provide cost effective 7 × 24 monitoring and security expertise. In this case, you may be up against a hard business decision, whereby they have already contracted an external organization to manage and monitor their logs and alerts, contracts have been put into place, and any attempt to take this over would be in conflict with their current business arrangements.

This could be a very unfortunate situation, as this may preclude you from including this server or server's log data in your centralized logging architecture, and thus exclude these log records from being part of your correlation effort, thus affecting your ROI from an analysis perspective. Although there may be the possibility to branch the log data off to your system, as well as the existing managed security service provider, they may see that as an affront to their system, and would not allow this to occur due to some possible exclusive rights in their contract. But this is why the survey is conducted: to find out these types of arrangements in advance to determine who may or may not be your customer candidates for your centralized logging approach.

## 7. If Stored Externally, How Are They Transported to the External Store (Syslog, FTP, Other)?

This question has to be answered if you do find that they are off-loading their logs to some server separate from the one generating the logs. You find out what this transport mechanism is, as there are many options in this space, some more standardized with easy integration capabilities and others much more difficult to work with and proprietary. Under the "standardized" category you may find that the system administrator has a syslog set up and you may be able to merely ask him to redirect this syslog method to your new centralized logging server or "collector," with little impact on his existing process.

However, you may also find cases where there is some funky propri-etary transport mechanism put into place that wouldn't be in your logging architecture and you will have to work with the system administrator to implement some more standardized data transport system to integrate into your architecture. Or in a worst-case scenario, the administrator has no interest in changing his processes or procedures in this area (from his proprietary transport method), and you either have to customize your system to meet his needs, or consider this a showstopper for him to participate in your consolidated logging effort, again an unfortunate situation, as your overall correlation capabilities will be affected by not having that aspect of data input.

And in rare cases you may actually find that due to previous audits or issues, they have been instructed to pay slightly more attention to security and have implemented some form of semisecure data transfer such as SFTP (Secure FTP, which it sometimes isn't if not done properly and has even had its share of exposed vulnerabilities on various operating system versions). Or some form of SCP (Secure CoPy) may be in place, but this begins to limit your options for integration into your process, as you may not have the flexibility to adopt these somewhat vertical transport methods, even though they are utilizing a good practice to protect sensitive log data as it is moved around your network. Your COTS solution may have its own proprietary data protection scheme, not compatible with those systems listed (SFTP and SCP).

Again, the point here is to determine how they are moving these files around the network and to where in the network (or possibly outside the network, but that is a whole different issue based on the previous discussion and much harder analysis questions are raised if this is found to be the case). For now, capture the methods that are in place today, and turn them into requirements for your system, as we do once we have completed the review of all the survey questions.

## 8. Is There a Separate Physical Interface over Which the Logs Are Distributed Out of the Box?

Here is an interesting question that warrants asking because sometimes your system administrators may surprise you in what they have in place within your network infrastructure. One such surprise you might find is a best practice where there is a separation of functions by physical network interfaces on a system. Under this scenario you may find a system that is "dual-homed" whereby it has one network interface for its production access to the corporate backbone and a separate network interface to a different portion of the enterprise network solely for the purpose of administrative access both inbound to the system, and outbound in the form of logs and alerts being sent out over this interface. The potential impact on your logging effort may be that this administrative interface may not be on the general enterprise network, and thus not readily

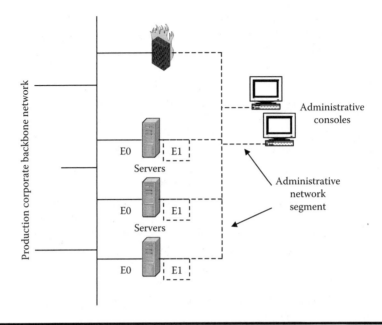

**Figure 3.1   Dual-homed systems for secure system administration**

available to send the log data to your enterprise located, consolidated logging server. Figure 3.1 illustrates this setup and why it can be considered a best practice from a network security administration perspective, but also could affect your ability to easily capture log data from a server set up under this type of configuration.

In this illustration, the three servers each have two network interfaces; the E0 network interface is the server connection to the corporate backbone, but no administrative access is allowed over this interface. The servers are configured to allow only administrative access over the E1 network interface coming off the right side of the servers in this illustration, where there are dedicated consoles on this administrative network. This administrative network is firewalled off from the main corporate network, so the general user community and associated connectivity would not have the capability to affect or adversely administer these production servers.

There are obvious security gains to this type of architecture, but it soon becomes apparent if you are implementing a consolidated logging approach where your consolidated logging server or collector sits on the corporate backbone in order to serve the broadest audience, that you may not easily be able to capture log data from servers under the architecture illustrated. One approach to take would be to determine what the logging method is on these servers (via one of the questions above), and determine if an additional single firewall rule could be put into the Administrative Server Network firewall, to allow this type of transport protocol to pass outbound from the administrative network to your centralized logging server or collector. This rule could become more complex if some proprietary method of data transfer is utilized or if the transport is solely UDP-based (which makes firewall rules considerably less secure to implement). Or there may be consideration to allow the log data to be sent out the E0 interface directly to the corporate backbone, if it can still be maintained that only inbound administrative access remains on the E1 interface, still maintaining the majority of their secure administrative architecture. Either one of these solutions would allow you to keep these servers as candidates for your consolidated logging effort, with minimal impact to the native server architecture.

One final note or question may come up: why not put the consolidated log server on the Administrative Network, which at a high level makes sense, but experience shows that these types of network segments may appear many times over. There could be four or five individual administrative segments, all separated from the corporate backbone; there usually isn't just one within an enterprise. Again, it becomes quite clear that you must conduct a thorough survey of your existing infrastructure, as what you find may surprise you (and affect your logging effort).

## 9. What Are the Access Control Mechanisms over Access to the Stored Logs?

Another one of those "if" questions: if you find that there are appropriate audit logs being saved either on the server itself or some external server, you must determine what protections are currently over these logs, as well as who should have and who actually has access to these logs. This determination is not just for a security review, but also to determine who may have access, even though they may not be intended viewers of the log, but by the fact that there may not be appropriate controls, various people or processes may be accessing these logs due to the lack of controls. If the logs are merely a file on the server, the file permissions must be reviewed to determine how tightly controlled access is to these log files. If the file is open to all, there could be various unknown accesses, some valid, which, when the logs are moved to a consolidated log server, these unknowns will no longer have access, and, therefore, who would have now been disconnected from their data source. On the other hand, you may find very restricted access to these logs (as it should be), and the end users are easily identified and can be directed to the new source if and when the logs are placed in the consolidated log server you are developing.

If the logs are currently in some form of external log storage device, the rules on this device must be reviewed, as one has to assume if they have an off-load server to hold logs, there are probably multiple systems storing their logs on this device. Now comes the question of whether there are log-specific access rules in place, or whether everyone who has system logs going to this server has access to all other logs on this server. Unfortunately, this is more common then not, in order to minimize the administration of all the potential access rules on a common server. Here again is another potential benefit from launching your consolidated logging effort: by reviewing these access rules, and turning it into a requirement for your design phase, you may provide or enhance the protection schemes over the access to this potentially sensitive data. The requirement on your COTS logging products would be "Discretionary Access Control, by User or Groups."

One other area may come to light when asking this question, which might also benefit your effort, and that comes in the case of the "managed security service" provider situation that was discussed earlier. In determining the access controls over the log data, if you find that the log data is sent out to a wholly external organization, you or the contacting part of your company should have the right to review the access controls over your data, even when it resides externally. This is a good exercise in determining exposures of your internal corporate system data and should be done on a regular basis; although, as a part of this survey, it gives you the opportunity to do this discovery and learn where or what protections are in place.

## 10. Who Reviews the Logs? At What Frequency?

This is another one of those questions where the answer is probably fairly predictable, probably "no one" and "rarely." The task of performing log reviews is far from a glamorous task, and many times the logging is performed just to check off the audit box that indicates that logs are kept in some form or fashion. If, in fact, your survey question does reveal that there is a target person or group of people tasked with conducting the log reviews, then this should be noted and confirmed, both with the individuals or groups, as well as against the data access controls and even potentially the data path, the manner in which these users or groups of users gain access to the logs, as your consolidated solution has to duplicate this method to minimize the impact on the end users (if there are any).

**Table 3.2  Data Classification Matrix**

|                     | *Public*                            | *Confidential*                                                              | *Secret*                                                        |
|---------------------|-------------------------------------|----------------------------------------------------------------------------|----------------------------------------------------------------|
| At rest, internal   | Clear text                          | Clear text                                                                 | Encrypted                                                      |
| In transit, internal| Clear text                          | Clear text                                                                 | Encrypted                                                      |
| At rest, external   | Clear text                          | Encrypted                                                                  | Encrypted                                                      |
| In transit, external| Clear text                          | Encrypted                                                                  | Encrypted                                                      |
| Access              | Uncontrolled                        | Controlled                                                                 | Controlled                                                     |
| Samples of          | Press releases PR data Product info | Product development info Employee data *System Log & Configuration* data    | Board minutes Merger & acquisition data Future financials      |

# 11. What Is the Data Classification of This Log Data (Company Secret, Confidential, Internal Use)?

This is a question that is often overlooked, but because this is a security initiative it cannot be ignored, especially in this case where large volumes of data are going to be consolidated into one centralized location. Hopefully your organization has a data classification scheme in their security policy or asset classification policy. This policy should have two or more identifying data classifications, at a minimum, Public and Company Owned or Company Confidential. These types of policies usually provide guidance on the nature of controls over the various data types specifying who can have access, how the data is handled, when it needs to be encrypted (if at all), and possibly samples of each type of data for each classification. Table 3.2 illustrates a sample data classification matrix made up of three data classifications.

A couple of points come out here that apply specifically to your log consolidation initiative. In this sample classification there are three data types defined: Public, Confidential, and Secret. For each classification it provides guidance on protection actions that must be taken depending on where the data is being handled. "At Rest, Internal" applies to data that is stored inside your corporate enterprise when it is "at rest," meaning stationary, such as on a server or in a database. "At Rest, External" applies to data when it is stored external to your enterprise and potentially higher security controls must be applied, such as it now must be encrypted.

Under this classification scheme, *System Log & Configuration* data is given as an example of "Confidential" data, and has specific security controls that must be applied. The two key issues are the requirements to encrypt the data if it is external to the enterprise and that it must have controlled access to the data wherever it resides. If your log consolidation system is dealing only with logs internal to your organization and is, of course, storing the data internal to the enterprise, then no encryption is necessary, but it does mandate that you have controlled access to this data. So, even though you may have conducted your survey over the various logs you plan to collect and found that there may not have been controlled access to the log data in its native server or source, we must apply access controls now, per the policy (and the existing system is obviously out of compliance with policy).

An interesting instance also now comes up in respect to system log files when dealing with a managed security service provider. If during the course of your survey you find that some systems, or groups of servers, are handing over system logs and alerts to this external provider, it would be interesting to see if they are following the policy and sending and storing them in an encrypted format.

Now this is purely a hypothetical data classification matrix, but it is not entirely off base from what actual data classifications look like and the recommended controls that should be put into place. It becomes fairly obvious for the need at least to review your policy, and determine whether the data you will be working with falls within a controlled access data classification; the last thing you would want to happen then is to have a security-led initiative fail to respect the data security policy. And depending on your policy, you may find you will have to select a COTS log consolidation tool that has the ability to apply encryption to the data or is compatible with an add-on data encryption technology.

## 12. Is There a Log Reporting System? How Are the Logs Accessed and Viewed? How Many People in the Organization Are Required to Have Access to These Logs?

Usually the answers here are fairly standard: there is little in the way of a formal log reporting system. It usually consists of a file system, possibly with some high-level query capability, and possibly a few canned reports that can be run against the stored logs. Or it's left to some sysadmin to merely run a grep on the log to look for keywords, error codes, or IPs under question. The fact that they have the logs stored for the requisite period of time, and they can be retrieved is enough to meet audit findings and the process is left at that.

As for people who require access to the logs, that is usually a fairly low number as well, usually due to the fact there is no easy method to gain access to the logs, so the audience of users is quite small. Also, this question is different from the previous one where it was asked who has access to the logs. As previously mentioned, there could be few if any controls over the log file; that may not be appropriate, but it might be what is in existence. Whereas this question is there to determine who actually requires access to the logs, not who has access to the log files. At the point of taking the initial survey you will most likely find a very small number of people who currently claim they require access to the log data. Through the course of your log consolidation project, once you put the logs into a consolidated format, with some degree of high-level COTS reporting system on top of the data, you may find you will get many more requests for access to the data, as it has now become more usable, accessible, and readable. This isn't to say that you should throw open all access; remember your data security policy may classify the data as Company Confidential, or Controlled, or some such classification that mandates access control mechanisms. Regardless, as this point, just collect the list of personnel claiming access requirements to the log data, wherever it resides.

## 13. What Is the Nature of the Reviews: Are Keywords Searched, Summaries, or Just High-Level Eyeing of the Log Data?

This survey question closely follows the previous one: based on who requires access, now you must determine how they access the data and what they do with it. There may be personnel who are assigned that task of reviewing the logs on a periodic basis; you merely need to know if they utilize specialized tools or processes. You will most likely find little existence of any specialized tools or methods, so anything you provide as part of your consolidated logging methodology will be an improvement, but it doesn't hurt to ask initially how they are conducting their log reviews today. In some cases you might find some rudimentary homegrown methods, such as canned scripts that are available to the mid-level analysts or possibly forensics investigators to run against saved logs, but these are usually as far as anyone goes in the way of log review tools.

# 14. Are There Additional Log Review, Storage, or Analysis Capabilities That You Would Like to Have over This Log Data? If So, What Are They?

This is a good open-ended question for the end of your survey because usually after going through these questions it generates some thought on their logs, and possibly how they could better utilize them. For some of the basic systems you will find little in the form of sophisticated log storage, archival, or review, so in some cases you'll just get a lot of "No" answers or, "Who knows." But once you finish surveying this type of administrator, they now might want to have some of the log capabilities as the ones they were just queried. As an example, when asked if they off-load their logs, with a response of "No," now they have the chance to respond that "Yes" they would like this capability, as well as the ability to grant read access to a variety of people, because maybe in the past they have fielded requests for access to their logs but due to the lack of sophistication of their current logging system, they couldn't satisfy this request. Now is their chance to verbalize their needs in the log consolidation and retention field.

## The Completed Survey

Once you have completed the survey of the candidate systems in Phase One, it is time to collapse all the responses, and try to understand or formulate your requirements based on this data input. The following is a hypothetical group of responses consolidated into one completed survey. This is used to build a sample requirements matrix to show you how the process can work (and has in the past for the development for such a system and later for the selection of a COTS system for deployment). Three systems (a, b, and c) were surveyed, specifically for their current logging practices with the following response:

1. What forms of logging do you currently perform on this device?
   a. Retain Activity logs
   b. Retain Access violation logs
   c. Capture restart logs
2. What is the volume, amount of data, collected in one 24-hour period?
   a. 40 Mb/day
   b. 5 Mb/day
   c. <1 Mb/day

3. What is your retention period; that is, how long do you keep retrievable logs?
   a. As much as fits into 300 Mb/drive, rolled over.
   b. 30 days
   c. 60 days
4. What are the formats for this retention? 30 days online, 30 days tape, 3 months CD?
   a. Online
   b. Online
   c. Online
5. What is the "write per second" timeframe? How many records per second are generated and logged?
   a. Unknown
   b. Unknown
   c. Unknown
6. Where are the logs stored today (locally on the box, locally on a nearby server)?
   a. Syslog server
   b. Local machine
   c. Local machine
7. If stored externally, how are they transported to the external store (syslog, FTP, other)?
   a. Syslog
   b. N/A
   c. N/A
8. Is there a separate physical interface over which the logs are distributed out of the box?
   a. No
   b. No
   c. No
9. What are the access control mechanisms over access to the stored logs?
   a. File protections
   b. File protections
   c. Don't know
10. Who reviews the logs? At what frequency?
    a. Assigned to system admin
    b. Assigned to system admin
    c. Available to whoever has need to know
11. What is the data classification of this log data (Company Secret, Confidential, Internal Use)?
    a. System log data not classified (according to system administrator)
    b. Unknown
    c. Unknown

12. Is there a log reporting system? How are the logs accessed and viewed? How many people in the organization are required to have access to these logs?
    a. No formal system; file search only when necessary. Access assigned to system administrator
    b. No log viewer. Access assigned to system administrator
    c. None. Available on request basis
13. What is the nature of the reviews: are keywords searched, summaries, or just high-level eyeing of the log data?
    a. Keyword searches when requested
    b. Keyword and scripted searches available when requested
    c. Reviews on an "as requested" basis
14. Are there additional log review, storage, or analysis capabilities that you would like to have over this log data? If so, what are they?
    a. Would like to set up or have available a more sophisticated off-load server, with better reporting capability and longer retention periods (believing that the corporate policy may mandate periods longer than what is currently being stored; the timeframe is driven by the amount of log data stored, not time). Would like to see someone else maintaining the store, and possibly provide an actual reporting system for log queries and reporting. Belief the forensics team would like a better analysis capability. At the last investigation, logs were merely FTPd to them for their analysis in whatever manner they could come up with.
    b. A separate log storage system would free up resources on the existing device. Some form of reporting system should be available when access to the logs is required; it should be simple to use without much in the way of training requirements.
    c. A third-party storage system would be helpful to eliminate this as a sysadmin task.

It is fairly obvious little attention was paid to logging, and probably a good guess that they haven't been audited for their logging practices, at least not during the tenure of the system administrators surveyed for this project. There are some procedures (using the term generously) in place for some forms of logging, probably for what they believe is the minimum in order to meet audit requirements. It is probably a good guess that not much in the way of hard requirements reviews were conducted prior to their turning on their various forms of logging; most likely these logs were just what was turned on when the system was first brought up and little else done since then. Regardless, let's assume these systems are targeted for the first phase of your consolidation system. Based on these inputs you could now start assembling your requirements for selecting a COTS system, but it would be little better than what is already being done today, other than providing a separate audit logging box.

Due to the fact you are (we hope) building an improved and "compliant" process, you should also, of course, consult your security policy for the actual logging requirements, and let's assume you come across with the following high-level requirements according to your policy:

- "All critical EDP processing systems must maintain a security audit trail of security-relevant system activities, including but not limited to: access violations, failed access attempts, privileged accesses and changes, date, and time stamp."
- "System administrators are responsible for the system configuration, management, maintenance, and audit log retention."
- "Critical EDP systems must maintain system logs and security audit logs for a period of 75 days in a retrievable format."
- "The audit department must have the ability to request and receive security audit logs in a readable format for all critical EDP systems."

If this is the policy for the systems that were surveyed, it is apparent that these systems were not set up in compliance with current requirements by these policy statements. None of them meet the retention period, and two of them apparently don't log at the appropriate level. But now that you have reviewed the policy and have the current state of the logging on your target systems for consolidation, you can build a better requirements list that meets both the needs of your current environment, as well as maintains compliance with your corporate policy. Through this combination, a modified requirements analysis matrix can be assembled to analyze available products or to build your requirements for the creation of an in-house system for audit log consolidation. (Correlation requirements haven't even been considered at this point; that will be a value-added benefit when the systems are combined; we speak more to this capability in Chapter 7.)

The requirements matrix in Table 3.3 is simply set up to list the requirements, provide a weight of importance for each requirement, and provide a scoring mechanism to cross-compare multiple products—in this case, COTS products available in the marketplace.

This type of requirements matrix can provide a good clean view of what you are attempting to do with respect to audit log consolidation (at least up to this point; there are plenty more requirements and capabilities that we want to put into the system, but for now we go with this short list). Some requirements are more along the want or nice-to-have category and thus are given weighted values on this list. As you can see, this

**Table 3.3  Audit Log Requirements Matrix**

| | | Product One | | Product Two | |
|---|---|---|---|---|---|
| *Requirement* | *Weight*[a] | *Score* | *Rating* | *Score* | *Rating* |
| Maintain 10 Gb of online log storage | 3 | | | | |
| Support up to 500 writes/second to central log database | 3 | | | | |
| Support syslog as an input method | 3 | | | | |
| Support additional input methods (FTP, CP) | 2 | | | | |
| Support receipt of encrypted data | 1 | | | | |
| Discretional access control over stored logs by user or groups of users | 2 | | | | |
| Flexible reporting system for log access, reviews, and investigation services | 3 | | | | |
| Ability to filter log records to field level prior to writing to database | 3 | | | | |
| Ability to set up canned reports and queries against stored audit records | 3 | | | | |
| Ability to report on trends and provide event summaries | 2 | | | | |
| Ability to archive audit records over 75 days (or some preset time period) | 3 | | | | |
| Flexible back-end database system (two or more options to meet local database areas of expertise) | 2 | | | | |

[a] Weights: 3 = must have feature/requirement; 2 = nice to have feature; 1 = extra bonus feature

weighted scale goes from 3 down to 1. Where a 3 puts the requirement up near the must have level, an item weighted as a 1 is farther down, because it would add value to the overall system, but not having it wouldn't be a showstopper for product selection. Then by taking this as your shopping list to the various vendors and getting their input to product capabilities, you can score each vendor's capability (or claimed capability) to meet each of these requirements. Based on what they said or indicate, you can score them along similar lines, where a 3 score indicates they fully meet the requirement, a 2 indicates a partial ability to meet the

**Table 3.4  Scored Requirements Matrix**

| Requirement | Weight | Product One | | Product Two | |
|---|---|---|---|---|---|
| | | Score | Rating | Score | Rating |
| Maintain 10 Gb of online log storage | 3 | 3 | 9 | 2 | 6 |
| Support up to 500 writes/second to central log database | 3 | 3 | 9 | 2 | 6 |
| Support syslog as an input method | 3 | 3 | 9 | 3 | 9 |
| Support additional input methods (FTP, CP) | 2 | 2 | 4 | 2 | 4 |
| Support receipt of encrypted data | 1 | 0 | 0 | 3 | 3 |
| Discretionary access control over stored logs by user or groups of users | 2 | 2 | 4 | 2 | 4 |
| | | | 35 | | 32 |
| | | Rating Summation | | Rating Summation | |

requirement, a 1 says they may offer the capability in a follow-on release, and a 0 score indicates they don't have the capability and it is not in their roadmap to offer that capability. You then take the scored value for each line item, multiply it by the weighted value for that requirement line item, and determine a calculated score. Table 3.4 illustrates a scored requirements matrix for two products for the first few line items in this matrix.

Product One meets most of the main requirements fully and thus scores a 3 for the first three line items. It only scores a 2 for the next line item of "Support additional input methods" possibly because it only offers one or two additional input methods, whereas the requirements list wanted to see many more, or at least more than two. Then the ability to support the receipt of encrypted data: it doesn't have this capability and there are no plans in the product roadmap to address this requirement, and thus it scores a 0. And finally in respect to supporting discretionary access control, it does have some ability in this area but not to a full extent and thus only scores a 2. Then the summation of the calculated scores for this product are totaled and listed at the bottom of the fourth column.

A similar scoring process is carried out for Product Two. It does not completely meet the first few line items; it meets the requirements at an acceptable level and thus scores 2s and a 3 here. An interesting feature of this scoring practice emerges with Product Two: even though it fully meets a line item that Product One misses (encryption), that alone is not enough to put it in the lead, because the encryption line item was a nice-to-have feature, and thus was not weighted as high; therefore, Product Two's ability to meet this low-weighted item didn't (and shouldn't) make it the clear winner.

We now see how we can build this requirements matrix based on the combined inputs of the target users of the consolidated logging system, as well as interpretations of our corporate audit logging requirements, and translate them into a numerically calculated scoring matrix against existing products serving this space.

We continue to use this product requirements matrix throughout this text, as we identify additional toolset features that we feel we need to enhance our project and probability of success in delivering an enhanced logging and reporting system to meet the enterprise security and audit needs.

A few more issues/items should be mentioned before we move on with the requirements matrix. Table 3.2 is based on just the few survey responses we obtained for our Phase One candidates, and the current corporate policy statements related to audit logging requirements. If you are going to make this a multiphase project, where you add systems farther down the road, then you should attempt to expand your requirements now based on some forecast of additional systems to add. It is a basic scalability issue, for those areas that will be affected by additional source inputs you will need to up the requirements. A few of the key line items that should be enhanced to address this potential scalability would be the data store size as well as the writes per second requirement. It would not be unrealistic to triple or quadruple the requirement for number of writes per second, given the vast potential of systems that you may want to correlate or consolidate into your system. As for data store size, you will find that it grows exponentially as you add systems. Take the current line item asking for a data store of just 3.7 gigabytes from the responses of data capture from just the three systems in Phase One. Table 3.5 illustrates this simple calculation for determining the data store needs for these three systems based on the current logging volumes (which we believe to be incomplete, but at least it gives us a starting point).

By taking the volumes indicated in the survey (40, 5, and 1 Mb a day) and assuming compliance to the corporate standard of 75 days worth of audit log data retained, we can calculate how much initial storage space the Phase One system will require. A more appropriate estimate might

**Table 3.5 Data Storage Calculation**

|  | *Daily Input (Mb)* | *Retention Period (Days)* | *Total Store (Mb)* |
|---|---|---|---|
| System a | 40 | 75 | 3000 |
| System b | 5 | 75 | 375 |
| System c | 1 | 75 | 75 |
|  |  |  | 3450 (or 3.4 Gb) |

be performed by just upping each system to the 40 Mb a day (the highest of all three systems), giving us 120 Mb a day multiplied by the 75-day retention period and we come up with 9 Gb of data storage if System One is at the appropriate level of logging in its generation of 40 Mb a day of log data.

This is where we now have to make the point to forecast out for growth and scalability in our requirements matrix, knowing that we plan to add systems and devices in follow-on phases of the initiative. Luckily the security audit logging marketplace is slowly beginning to mature and is adding the ability to not only address very large data stores, but many are also incorporating high data compression schemes into their data store, some claiming up to a 10:1 ratio between actual data and real storage (where they claim 100 terabytes of "actual" data can be stored in only 10 terabytes of real storage space).

We have now clearly pointed out that the initial survey estimates only a small portion of the total volume that your log consolidation system will have to address over time. At best, you can make long-range broad forecasts, but at least you know that you have growth and expansion expectations and can make those requirements to the vendor when you go into the evaluation and selection process. And as experience has shown, it is literally, "If you build it, they will come." The author is now experiencing a global syndrome of "Take my audit log, please."

And what forecast isn't complete without a forecast chart. Leveraging off what we know or think we know from our three application servers, we've estimated, if set at the appropriate level of logging, they produce 40 Mb of data a day. Then we survey at least two of the other candidate servers that we plan to expand our consolidated logging effort into, such as firewalls, and we find an appropriately configured audit log for one day generates 80 Mb a day, and an appropriately configured RADIUS authentication server generates 35 Mb a day. We now have the benchmarks to do our "over time" forecast data store requirements. We estimate how long it might take to fold in these additional devices, say, in three-month intervals (which experience shows, is probably fairly accurate given the

**Table 3.6  Cumulative Data Storage Calculation**

| Device | Mb/Day | No. Devices | Total Data Store × 75 (Gb) | Cum. Log Server (Gb) | Quarter |
|---|---|---|---|---|---|
| Applic. server | 40 | 3 | 9 | 9 | 1st |
| Firewalls | 80 | 3 | 18 | 27 | 2nd |
| RADIUS servers | 35 | 3 | 7.8 | 35 | 3rd |
| Applic. server | 40 | 3 | 9 | 44 | 4th |

politics, technical issues, and product capabilities to address heterogeneous data input devices for logging). Table 3.6 illustrates a pencil forecast of adding groups of systems every three months and the effect on your cumulative data storage requirements.

Even as high-level estimates, they clearly indicate the high growth rate, and need for a system that can handle these volumes of data not only for mere storage, but also, as we mature the system, it can handle these volumes for the reporting, queries, and eventually event correlation, a key component of the end system being implemented.

On a final note of data collection for requirements formation, a more formal process could be initiated to conduct a formal assessment, but the cost and time to execute are probably not within the financial boundaries of your initiative. What can be done though is to go back to previous assessments, audits, and evaluations of the enterprise and review these reports specifically for any findings or "observations" in respect to audit logging. It is usually low hanging fruit from an auditing perspective, so you are sure to find a couple of systems that were found to be out of compliance and thus are ideal candidates for your consolidation effort which will be put into place in a corporate compliant manner (remember you actually went back and reviewed the section of the corporate audit policy addressing this aspect). Another good research area would be your "waivers from compliance" file if you can gain access to it through the appropriate channels. In many organizations, for every rule, there's a documented process to break the rules; this is usually a waiver process of some form or fashion. It is here that the systems that were found to be out of compliance have filed for and been granted a waiver from compliance, or systems that knowingly went into production out of compliance but due to time constraints or resources, were able to file for and get approval through the waiver process to proceed.

By reviewing these lists you can potentially get an idea of your forecasted customer list, as anyone not in audit log compliance can usually only remain in that phase for a set period of time, and either have to correct it, or continue to renew the waiver.

So, we now have a start on our requirements list based on preliminary surveys of our current state, extrapolations of potential growth areas and volumes, and have begun to take into account what the possible effects various survey responses will have in our developing consolidation architecture. The charts and calculation charts should be freely used in your own estimations and calculations. In the next chapter we delve deeper into the specifics of the system and its technical requirements based on enhanced capabilities in the data correlation arena. Here, we merely began setting up the system basics. Easy, right?

# Chapter 4

# Deciding What to Capture and How to Do It

At this point, you have decided to move forward, either with an enterprise log consolidation and trace log analysis program, or with enhancements to the existing program. If you have chosen the enhancements route, you have, it is hoped, thoroughly surveyed the program and now have a good handle on its "current state" with respect to your logging processes (or lack thereof). You should have also identified what your specific requirements are, either from an external regulatory agency or board, your own company's policies, or industry-specific requirements. Your program should also have been modified to perform a full capture of the audit log records, which will be used later for full audit log compliance, as well as potentially for computer security forensics or after-the-fact investigations. Alternatively, you may have decided that your logging will be used solely for the purposes of audit log alerting, or alarms in a consolidated fashion, but we touch more on that approach in Chapter 5 and beyond.

Starting with the target full log capture, correlation, and storage for computer forensics, you now have a very high level, target goal and objective. You are now ready to collect log records from multiple network and security devices, but will likely want to perform some form of filtering (more on this later). Then you will store the data either in one common database, or in multiple linked databases. Against this database, you will then select a correlation engine, assign correlation rules, and either run, or program to run, correlation reports for alerting at a high level. At this point, you will also be able to provide query capabilities against the aggregated data either through canned queries or with ad hoc queries, depending on who your user base is and their access capabilities. With this said, let's dive into the multistep process and explore each step in more detail. We begin by defining what you are going to capture and from where, keeping in mind that the goal is to perform the computer forensics and audit log compliance.

## Requirements Gathering for Whole Log Capture

It is recommended that the data collection efforts be started on a small scale and with those logs from common or easily accessible sources. Given that this effort is probably being initiated by the information security group, the targeted logs for capture should probably be related to security devices, as stated previously, starting with possibly a small number of firewalls. The firewall logs that you start with may be from your most prominent or critical access point(s), such as your Internet gateway(s) or partner gateways. When you do choose to capture these logs, after having completed the survey (as stated in the previous chapter), these logs should be examined closely to determine what level of logging is currently invoked, as many firewalls have various logging levels, with the lowest levels capturing minimal data in most cases. In fact, these captures can be so minimal that the data is of little use for any type of thorough analysis—forensic or otherwise. However, experience shows that configuration by nonsecurity personnel usually results in settings at the lowest level of logging, with the intention of promoting the efficiency of the firewall (under the assumption that the more log records cut, the less efficient the firewall becomes).

If you find the firewall log to be deficient in its logging (i.e., at a very low level, with only minimal information being relayed), then it is time to perform an in-depth review of the logging capabilities of that particular firewall. However, be careful not to jump immediately to the other extreme and demand that the logging be increased to its highest level. Ideally, the logging level should be incrementally increased one notch at a time. Each logging level should be run for a period of time, with the log from each period being examined by a senior information security analyst to determine the usefulness of the logged data. If the data appears to be useful for forensic, system, or security purposes, then it is worthwhile to move on to the next higher level, until a level is reached where no additional useful data can be extracted. It is also highly recommended that you run the actual log level and not just review the manual and what is provided by sample reports. From an analysis perspective, nothing works better

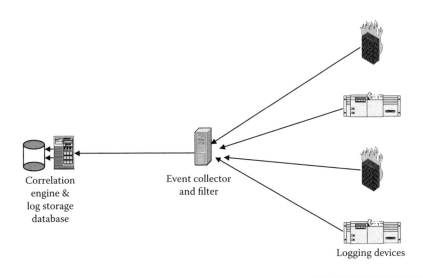

**Figure 4.1    Three-tier log consolidation architecture**

than your own log data, which contains network names, users, sessions, IP ranges, and so on, which are familiar to you and your information security analysts.

In addition, when performing this analysis you may draw the conclusion that you have reached a level of logging that provides too much data, or superfluous records, whereas the next level down provides too little data. This is not quite the dilemma it appears to be as nearly all vendor-supplied products that you evaluate will have the capability to filter out individual log records during the collection cycle. With this in mind, the recommendation is to set the firewall logging level at one level higher than necessary in order to have the higher number of records, so that this filtering will bring you down to the number of data/fields that you wish to record. This filtering usually takes place in the middle layer of the three-tiered log consolidation architecture depicted in Figure 4.1.

As you can see, the choice of what to log or capture becomes somewhat of a balancing act between capturing all the data and possibly too much, or capturing too little data. Capture too much and you run the risk of needing very high storage requirements for data that may never be used. Capture too little and you risk the possibility of missing key information that you may not have realized you needed until it is missing. This may be the case, for example, when the decision must be made whether to capture vendor unique error codes, or device error numbers, which at first may appear unimportant, but later you may realize that your only reference or key to a particular event is by the unique vendor-supplied code. You may have chosen to omit it or filter it out because you saw little value in it at the time you were first designating the records and fields to retain in your logging system. For this reason when you work with your database administrator or vendor on the configuration of your particular database store architecture, it may be worthwhile to insert some spare fields so that at some point in the future, you can add additional key fields that may not have been originally designed into the system to be captured but were previously filtered out.

Although this task of filtering may appear to be tedious, in many product cases, there are built-in "normalizers" that perform this data collection from the endpoint devices and then push, write, or send the normalized or standardized data to the back-end database and correlation engine. Here, the explanations can be found to provide a more complete understanding of the process and to provide the background should some degree of internal analysis have to be performed on the normalization process.

At this point, you have designated the firewall(s), from which you plan to capture logs. You have analyzed the logging that was performed by each of the firewalls and you have established the appropriate level of logging to be performed at that device. Now, the decision must be made as to how best to send the log data to your collection point or server. Assuming a commercial off-the-shelf (COTS) application set, you will most likely have an intermediary collection device (see Figure 4.1) that will collect the logs directly from the firewall(s), and possibly perform the filtering we spoke of earlier, as well as normalize the data into your consolidation log server's overall standard format. First we take a look at the processes of transferring the data and then go into more detail on the normalization process.

Common transport mechanisms can be utilized to move the log data from the end device into your log collection architecture (syslog or more current syslog_ng), or custom transport mechanisms can also be used. Each approach has its costs and benefits, with the costs not necessarily being in real dollars, but rather in time and resources.

The benefit of utilizing a common method such as syslog is that it is easily implemented. It only requires a minor change at the endpoint (the firewall from which the logs are being captured) and it should not cause too much work for the overworked device administrator. But, an issue does emerge over the sensitivity of the log data, and the concern of sending it "in the clear," unencrypted from the end device. One school of thought maintains that the single log is not sensitive enough on its own, and is only useful for a "slice in time," hence the reduction in sensitivity. In many cases, however, this is the norm, and is procedurally accepted. It also depends on where the end firewall (or other device) is located on your network and what the data path is from that device back

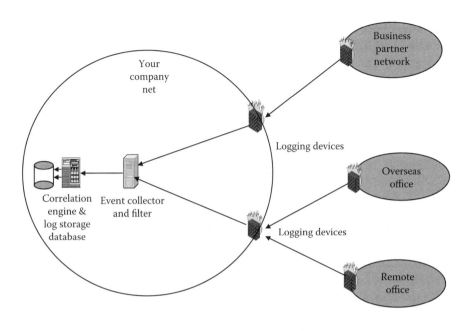

**Figure 4.2    Extended endpoints of log sources**

to your collection point. If it is all on the interior of your intranet and you have a high degree of confidence that you have a closed system, then possibly the syslog approach would be the best and easiest implementation. However, if the end device is on the far perimeter/outer reaches of your infrastructure (such as at a satellite office), or overseas, or in some other higher-risk area, then syslog with clear text sends may not be the optimal solution from a security perspective. See Figure 4.2 for a depiction of the various potential areas of risk in respect to log collection. This is where consideration of the alternatives of encrypted collection should be evaluated or considered.

The alternative is to implement some form of secure transport, which is commonly available in the COTS log collection applications, although this usually requires that their software agent be placed on the end device, and some form of keying be implemented to support the encryption. The software agent is usually keyed with some form of encryption, which is performed at the end device through this code and only then sent to the log collection device, possibly with a proprietary transport of its own, or syslog, but now also with an encrypted file, for which only the log collection device has the paired key (symmetric or asymmetric, depending on the application's design for encryption; most utilize symmetric keys for simplicity).

But, this now requires the administrator of the end device to go beyond a configuration adjustment; i.e., she must now also install this agent software and learn how to configure it, and be assured that there will be little impact on the system. Proof of this will, of course, require a pilot test on the development or lab version of the firewall, which must be configured in exactly the same manner as the production version all the way down to the operating system and patch level. This also requires that your selected log collection application support this end device with the appropriate agent, and the operating system of the endpoint be supported (and that it is not so old that the agent isn't compatible), and that the box has the processing cycles available to support another small executable (how many of your current devices have plenty of extra processing horsepower?). In the author's experience, many of these logging agents consist of small code (intentionally so, in an attempt to minimize the impact on the end device). But occasionally this low-level code can lack the necessary sophistication and in some cases overall compatibility, which leads to errors in installation and, in turn, results in less then optimal error coding and debugging.

It quickly becomes obvious that careful scrutiny must be applied when making the decision to go agent-based or nonagent-based, as the extra testing and effort required for the agent-based approach can be considerable. In fact, the decision process should be conducted well ahead of the selection of the product because if you do realize the need to utilize agents for collection of your logs from your various endpoints, then you must ensure that the COTS product you select supports the majority of devices that you have in mind. Not only should it be able to support your target endpoints for log collection, but it should also offer an option to support custom agents for possible strange endpoints that may exist in your network. You might just feel the need to collect the log from this device, strange device, or version (do you still have that Checkpoint v2.0 firewall running in that satellite office in Paducah, KY?).

Part of the up-front analysis as previously stated is to identify your target log sources in your network. This should include the various phases of your project, with the hope that you start out with a limited number of devices in order to simplify the initial implementation. You may then choose to expand it over time to other devices and functions. But, it is from the initial analysis that you should derive the various devices you intend to collect from, as well as come up with a list, and the breadth, of devices, to use for questioning the vendors regarding their ability to provide an agent or some form of encryption for each of these devices. This is in case you should decide to use that as part of your log collection process, agent-based encrypted transport. You will also need to decide whether to encrypt the log collection based on your own standards with respect to what the log data classification is per your security policy, or "asset classification" (in this instance, "asset" being data). This step of the analysis will also indicate whether there is a need per your own policy to encrypt the log data as it traverses your defined data path back to your log collection server. You may find that both by policy and potentially by the controlled data path there is little risk to the data, and thus the requirement to encrypt via available agents becomes a moot point. However, it wouldn't hurt to put it down as a low-level specification on your KTA requirements matrix as a "nice to have" feature of the COTS products being considered.

Once this process is completed, the next step is to take this case of your log collection proposal and tools to your auditors to get confirmation that your findings are correct (whether to encrypt or not to encrypt). A common issue at this step is that you may find that your interpretation of the policy, and your logic, may vary greatly from theirs. If, for example, you have chosen not to encrypt then this may be in conflict with their analysis of the situation. If this is the case and you have not initially presented it to your auditors then at some point after implementation you may wake up to an audit finding over your whole architecture, for not encrypting what they may have deemed to be sensitive data. The point here is that it is important to have your analysis well documented, and have the presentation to the auditors in a documented format (even if it is as simple as meeting minutes of your conversation with date, time, and an attendees list).

If you use a third-party audit team, this becomes a little trickier for a couple of reasons. One, it may be costly to have them come in to do the analysis; and, two, when third parties are utilized, today's third-party audit team, may not be tomorrow's third-party audit team. As a result, you will run the risk that if you are conducting this analysis before product selection or implementation, by the time the next audit comes around, the new audit team may be on site and have completely different interpretations. Thus, it is imperative to have some form of up-front analysis, communication of your findings and solution, and documentation of agreements of your architecture if for no better reasons than to cover your assets!

## The Normalization Process

Now that we have reached the point of actually pinpointing the data to be collected as well as the sources and access path, we progress to the second tier of the three-tier audit log collection architecture. In this tier, there is usually a "collection" server which has multiple functions in the overall architecture. One of the primary functions of the collection server

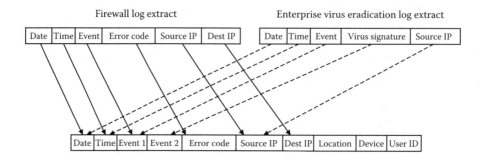

**Figure 4.3   Normalization of log events**

is to reduce the load on the back-end device as part of the overall log collection process. In large-scale architectures there are multiple collection servers, either by geography or endpoint collection devices (one collector for firewalls, one for authentication servers, one for network device logs, etc.). But in addition to functioning as a mere physical collection point, they also perform the normalization process, which is the collection and formatting of the data into a standardized structure before writing or sending it to the main collection point and database.

This normalization process is the act of taking in the dissimilar logs and putting them into the common fields of the consolidation server. Figure 4.3 depicts a simplistic normalization of a few records from a firewall device and an enterprise virus eradication server. Some fields are common and thus are placed into the same, named field, and, if necessary, formatted to a common format. A field such as "Date" may come in mmddyy, or mmddyyyy, or ddmmyy, in which case the normalization process would perform a standardization from the source log into a defined common format before it is written to the core database. As an example, your firewall may have 26 fields in its logging record, and some fields are common to many of the devices you are collecting from, and thus should all be put in the same common field in the consolidated server(s). Such common fields would be:

- Time of Event
- Date of Event
- Event ID or Error Code(s)
- Source IP Address
- Destination IP Address
- Device Identifier(s) (host name of the firewall or IP address)
- User/Device/ID

You would probably find all these same fields in your router logs, virus eradication server, proxy logs, SPAM filter, authentication server(s), and other network devices in the path of data flows. Again, an up-front analysis should be performed to determine the correct placement and normalization of the individual record fields into your master consolidated database. Issues can arise if each of the fields in the end device is not fully understood. One group or category of fields that has caused issues in past such exercises, is the multitude of "message ID" fields. In multiple log analysis exercises we have found that out of 26 fields, there may be two or more that have some sort of message ID number. Sometimes we have found them to be hierarchical, which explains why there are multiple fields of "message ID," but by mistakenly only taking the lower-level number in the hierarchy, we had duplicate numbers, which was not actually the case. They actually had different "family" numbers one level up. Table 4.1 better depicts the issue here, and why care must be taken when deciding what to filter out. Note how the "Event2" field has multiple values of "100," which if sorted alone would appear to be the same event, whereas they are actually subsets of "Allows and Denies," further showing the need to capture all fields in certain cases to address hierarchical details of logging.

It should be obvious by now that a high degree of analysis must be performed when looking at the data to be collected, and it must be done down to the field level on each device from which you plan to collect logs. Also, it is important to note how it is placed in the normalized database. This task can be thought of as the mapping of fields from the end device to the larger database. A good analogy of this is the configuration of the synchronization between your PDA and desktop if you have ever performed that function on the Palm device, where you map the calendar fields on your desktop to the calendar fields on your PDA. They may not be a precise match so in some cases you have to interpret or make decisions on where to place like fields. Despite the fact that many of the COTS products in the logging and collection arena have normalizers for just this task, it is important to understand their function and methodology. These normalizers are usually designed specifically for a wide variety of endpoint devices specific to the manufacturer, and even as specific as the version, as we have experienced vendors who have changed their logging format as newer versions emerge, or underlying operating systems change. For example, in the case of a Cisco acquisition of a product and as part of the integration into the Cisco family of products, Cisco migrated the device to the Cisco IOS operating system, eliminating its native operating system, resulting in a change to the original log formatting. This last example highlights the importance of the need to be fully aware of all changes in your log feeds from version upgrades to

**Table 4.1  Field Hierarchy Collection**

| Date | Time | Event1 | Event2 | Error Code | Source IP | Dest IP | Location | Device | UserID |
|------|------|--------|--------|-----------|-----------|---------|----------|--------|--------|
| 4-Sep | 21:40 | Deny | 100 | A1 | 10.72.5.1 | 129.197.3.1 | FW1 | Gtway | N/A |
| 4-Sep | 21:42 | Deny | 100 | A1 | 10.72.5.1 | 129.197.3.1 | FW1 | Gtway | N/A |
| 4-Sep | 21:43 | Allow | 100 | B1 | 10.72.8.5 | 198.5.3.2 | FW1 | Gtway | Jsmith |
| 4-Sep | 21:44 | Allow | 100 | B1 | 10.72.8.4 | 198.5.5.4 | FW1 | Gtway | Pjones |

product acquisitions and to recognize that your log inputs will change over time (usually at the most inopportune time).

In addition to the normalization process, the "event collector" can also be used to perform filtering of the data prior to writing it to the main repository or correlation engine. Because the event collector is receiving the data directly from the endpoint, it has all the raw data and, as previously mentioned, this can be more then you intend to keep, but because of the lack of precise logging capabilities at the endpoint, you were forced to initially capture more than you intended. In this case, you can program the event collector to filter out events or record types that you don't want to keep in the long run, and only pass on the records targeted for your consolidated logging effort in your master database. However, once again, some degree of analysis must be performed if you are going to perform any filtering, as you may end up eliminating data records that could affect your ability to perform forensic investigations.

There are some fields, though, that can readily be eliminated, such as any records that merely showed activity, such as "keep alive" messages. For example, we found that one system actually logged such events, which could be used for debugging purposes, but here they were merely extraneous records in normal logging routines. One would hope that the end device had enough discretionary log settings that such events could be filtered out at the end device and not at your filter, but just in case this option was not available, your event collector can be utilized to perform just this type of filtering. It can also be utilized to optimize your architecture: by minimizing the data where you can, you will reduce the overall burden of storage and the amount of data being transported across your network.

Once again, the main thing to remember is to scrutinize the process, in the event that you later choose to invoke some form of filtering. This is done to prevent relevant data from being lost, and highlights the constant need to balance your design between optimization and thorough capture of relevant data. Also, recognize that this may be an interactive process. After enabling the filter, you may want to "over-capture" the data in the beginning. Next, take readings as to how quickly you are acquiring data over the coming days or weeks. This information will be useful for forecasting the total storage requirements for the required retention period. If you find that there is a need for data reduction then the data is there for analysis and, depending on your findings, you can then invoke some form of filtering solely for the purpose of data reduction. However, take care to note what you are "reducing out" in the interest of optimization.

The next critical step is to engineer the placement and number of collectors. The three-tier architecture depicted is made up of the end device, event collector(s), and back-end correlation and reporting structure, which is common to the product arena for log collection and correlation or what are now commonly known as SEMs, Security Event Managers. In addition to providing the normalization function and filtering function, the event collector also acts as a physical collection point from your disparate end devices across your network. In larger environments, multiple collectors are required or recommended in order to spread out the load and make distributing collection of the log inputs more efficient so as not to overload any given device. Even if the first phase only warrants a single collector, it is still important to map out a strategy for the placement of your collector(s), from the first through the $n$th collector, where $n$ is the value you require for scalability across your enterprise.

One typical approach is to place collectors near the greatest number of devices, regardless of the type of device, and up to some percentage of the collector's capacity. The collection capacity of the event collector varies on the COTS specifications which can also be variable based on the amount of functions being performed by the collector, such as normalization and filtering, which is why that analysis has to be completed prior to selecting and placing the number of collectors. A high amount of processing on the collector will, of course, reduce its capacity to collect the raw log data from the end devices and may be cause to co-locate multiple collectors at the same point.

If you do end up placing two collectors co-located, there is another decision to be made in their processing and record collection. Murphy's law says that first there will be an odd number of devices at the endpoint that you have to collect from so it won't be an easy division of devices per collector, so you'll end up with something like five high-volume devices in one location.

Next you need to decide whether to simply divide the devices between the two collectors: two report to collector #1 and three report to collector #2 as depicted in Figure 4.4. Under this scenario you hope that no one device exceeds the capacity of the single collector, as the other collector won't be of any help. The more advanced method is to implement a load-balancing architecture such that both collectors share the task of capturing data from all five systems, but this requires additional hardware and planning, though it also provides the greatest benefit in being able to handle spikes in data being sent from any one of the five devices. Figure 4.4 also depicts the load-balanced architectural approaches for co-locating event collectors where you have a concentration of high-volume devices feeding logs into your consolidated logging architecture. The additional benefit is that you can scale the load-balanced architecture even further by adding event collectors behind the load-balancer as the need arises, adding capacity that can be applied to all these devices, although this

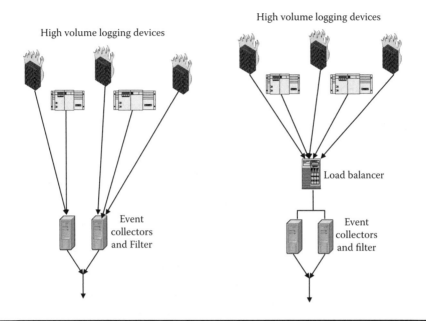

**Figure 4.4  Co-located event collectors**

assumes that the next high-volume device will be geographically close to this implementation.

Getting back to the normalization process that takes place on these collectors, in analyzing a collector with respect to functions, we can assume that some degree of normalization is obviously being performed on the data coming in from each endpoint. Additionally, for the purpose of estimating capacity we can assume some degree of filtering may be occurring, but not to any great extent, as filtering is usually the exception, not the rule, for most of the raw data collection.

Having covered the first two functions, let's look at the raw data capture, vis-à-vis the decision on the number of event collectors and their placement. One more variable to consider is the efficiency of data throughput. Once again, there are variables that are worthy of consideration for both initial and long-term deployment. Assuming the event collector is doing some filtering, this would indicate that more data is entering the filter than exiting, so the assumption is that the filter is removing data. Therefore, the more efficient data path would be on the downstream side of the event collector. This would dictate that you place the event collectors close to the end devices that are feeding into the raw data logs. The thinking here is that the end device may be sending too much data as a result of its inability to pare down the data, hence, you are relying on the event collector to perform this function. Figure 4.5 illustrates the

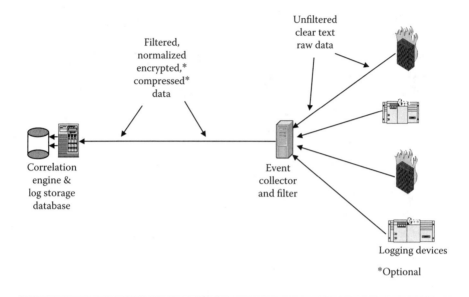

**Figure 4.5   Factors influencing event collector placement**

influential factors in placing your event collectors in your enterprise. As we discuss later, the factors include the potential higher volume of unfiltered traffic from the end device going to the collector, as well as the clear text aspect, versus the filtered potentially lower volume of data leaving the collector and possibly sending encrypted traffic directly to the central repository.

Another consideration for the event collector placement returns us to the issue of encryption and the discussion of the potential need to encrypt the data flowing to the central collection mechanism from the remote endpoints from which we were collecting logs. Although we may have veered away from this before, we may still have some capability of encrypting from the event collector to the central database. This could provide a degree of risk mitigation by at least encrypting the data path from the event collector to the central repository (see Figure 4.5). This also gives us the benefit of not having to place an agent on the remote endpoint, as the encryption would be performed on the event collector itself. Granted, this is not a complete solution, but it should at least be considered as a risk mitigation technique. The risk mitigation would be increased the closer the event collector can be placed to the device generating the logs. If, for example, you are collecting from one Internet gateway and are able to place your event collector in the same physical rack and switch as the firewall(s), then this would be as reasonably close to the device as possible. This would greatly reduce the data path of unencrypted log data. So with these factors considered, it makes sense to try to place the event collectors as close as possible to the majority of the end devices that will be submitting log data into your system if your goal is to reduce the threat of cleartext log data being transferred across your network.

There are also issues to be taken into account regarding the function of encryption that should be raised with the vendor. These issues include: how much overhead does the encryption introduce into the processes being performed on the event collector and on the receiving central server? Also, how is the keying done to enable the encryption: that is, is it manual or automated? If manual, is it worth the effort? Also, what is the level of encryption? If it is at a very low level then, again, is it worth the additional effort? Finally, there is the internal discussion to be held as to whether it should be done at all. If your policy analysis indicates that it isn't necessary, and by doing so, the only added benefit is another, minor risk mitigation factor, then you must ask how much risk is being reduced. Because this would only occur over your internal lines (assuming your event collector is already within your boundaries), the higher risk data path would still lie on the upstream side of the event collector, for the raw data coming in from the endpoints. Therefore, some might argue that the encryption is in the "wrong place." To this point, your only reply can be that it is just an additional risk-mitigating step, and is not required. Again, this is merely a consideration, and a question of risk and performance management. Every enterprise is different, and the answer will depend upon the circumstances of each case. The important item is to understand the risks (data paths of sensitive data) and know what options are available to mitigate these risks.

Returning to the decision process for determining the location of the event collector, we have now covered some of the more pertinent factors that will affect the throughput and performance capability of the event collector. Assuming you can get reliable performance statistics from the vendor, and are able to factor in your collection requirements, you can now begin to estimate the number of collectors required for the initial infrastructure, and lay out plans for growth as your logging requirements expand.

Assuming the vendor provides data capacity rates in kilobytes per second, you are now equipped with a benchmark by which to rate your collection of logs from your remote points. Initially, this will only be a rough estimate of the output at the end devices, but after the initial burn-in period, you can expect to see more accurate counts. However, you should be able to make an initial estimate just by observing the raw log size of the end device over a given period of time and estimating the average volume as well as available link speed.[1] As you aggregate the total volume of data coming from all your planned initial endpoints, you should compare this number with the estimated capacity of your chosen vendor's event collector (or if you have done this before selecting the product, you now have a "minimum requirements" line item for your KTA matrix). A good rule of thumb is to not allow it to run more then 60 to 70 percent of the capacity of the event collector and possibly less if there are other high-volume processes targeted for the event collector and its data (encryption, filtering, etc.). Additionally, you may have to take into consideration data spikes of input from your endpoints. If you are collecting from a stable source, such as an authentication server, which cuts short records and may have some spikes during key log-on periods, this should not cause a major impact. But if you are capturing logs from a large Internet gateway firewall, which may be the main gateway for the corporation, then it is more likely to have spikes in logging just due to its nature and because it is a focal point. If the latter is the case, you may want to lower the threshold for aggregate capacity and only load it to 50 percent of the event collector's capacity to allow for data spikes or consider the load-balancing architecture previously described.

Another factor to be considered, in addition to the amount of data hitting the collector from your various endpoints, is the placement of the collector on the network. Also, you should observe the line (and line-speed) available and note how much traffic exists on that line today. These are questions that should be taken up with your network group, but you should also be prepared with all the previously identified data figures as they will be critical in sizing your network requirements.

It should be readily apparent by now that there are many factors that must be taken into account with respect to the sizing and placement of your event collectors. You must have the vendor-supplied data on the capacity and functional issues of the event collector itself, as well as the endpoint data/statistics in order to make your design decisions. Below is a summary of the key questions that should be asked of the endpoint device manager. Refer to the paragraphs above to review the issues surrounding these questions. In some cases, the device manager may not have the exact answers, so expect to have to estimate them on the first go-round.

1. How large is the average log size over one 24-hour period?
2. What is the largest log collected in one 24-hour period?
3. What are the average and highest log messages per second or per minute?
4. What is the average logging rate (kbps)?
5. What is the highest recorded logging rate (kbps)?
6. What is the data classification of the log data?

So far, we have focused purely on the technical side of event collector placement, but keep in mind there are other significant factors separate from the technical arena. You may find that certain business units may want to have a completely separate reporting or logging approach. This could be the case, for example, for either high-value or high-risk environments such as development labs, which are physically or logically separated from the main backbone network infrastructure. From both design and security perspectives, it makes sense to place an event collector directly in these cordoned-off areas, as there is usually a firewall between these special areas, or zones, and the corporate backbone. Instead of opening multiple additional holes in the firewall from each of the endpoints to the event collector, it would be easier to simply place the event collector in the zone that is cordoned off, and then open a single port in the firewall from just the single event collector to the central collection server, thereby minimizing the exposure and impact on the firewall.

The other nontechnical decision when placing event collectors may focus on data type. If you have an environment that is part of your actual product, such as Web hosting services and this is the bread and butter of your organization, the logs of this environment are, of course, of utmost importance and criticality. Versus the logs of just your internal corporate architecture or desktop environment, they may not warrant the scrutiny and timeliness of your product environment. In this case you may want to have separate event collectors, one for your product environment/hosting side and another one for your device logs covering your corporate infrastructure/desktop environment, internal to your organization. This also provides a natural load-balancing architecture, whereby the high volumes of your product environment can be built up and scaled for that environment and a smaller, less-in-demand environment can be installed for your internal corporate architecture.

Other issues surrounding the placement of the event collector are usually specific to the geographical region and reflect the need to keep the regional or geographically located devices on the same collector. This is usually due to smaller long-haul links between geographically dispersed sites, and thus the need to consolidate the raw logs first before sending them over potentially bandwidth-constrained long-haul links. And in a worst-case scenario for far-reaching sites, they may require a complete mini-installation, comprised of the event collector and a local data repository and correlation engine. This raises yet another product requirement for your product selection criteria. Does the system offer different sized implementations with corresponding pricing? For flexibility you should not select a company that only offers the $200K "Enterprise Product," as it would not give you smaller product deployment options should you need to build out a single site with its own log consolidation architecture due to geography, separation of business lines, or link communication issues. If you do make this a hard requirement, then you should also require some form of "tiered hierarchy" either for the management or reporting between a remote site implementation and your core enterprise implementation. The reason being, if you do end up building a smaller architecture out at a remote site, you would still want some degree of tie-in and commonality over all implementations of the product. You would want them to be able to leverage off the core reports written at your central site and scripted to the same format as well as having standard management practices.

This tiered product hierarchy should include the ability to push out standard configuration parameters from the central site to remote installations, to leverage off central policies and report development. The remote site installations should also enable central management as an option for complete management of the remote site by central personnel via a remote user management console function. Of course, there should still be the flexibility to allow localized management, but with the ability to receive configuration updates from the central site. The other side of the distributed architecture should allow for the roll-up of reports from the remote sites into the central infrastructure to provide some form of a single view of the enterprise from a security-reporting perspective. This doesn't say that all remote data is sent to the central site, only that reports generated at the remote site from the same script can be rolled up to the central site and incorporated in the reporting numbers. An example of this may be the Firewall Deny report. If the same script that generated this report is run at the remote installation against their border firewalls, and numbers come up, this report can be rolled up into the central site, and because it has the same report parameters and output fields, it can be included in the central Firewall Deny report, reflecting the remote site numbers. This ensures the ability to establish a standardized logging and reporting structure in a highly distributed environment.

So now we have the base requirements for the placement of the logging infrastructure components with some degree of understanding of some of the influencing factors for the placement of these components in the enterprise. Once this is done during the initial design of your architecture, you can develop an ongoing template for expansion of your system. The initial rollout may not be the long-standing architecture; you may have to do some refinements once you learn the capabilities of your system. However, once these parameters are identified and documented, you can then develop a template for future growth. This template will help you plan just how many event consolidators are required, whether to place them local to the devices or use existing event collectors, what their capacity is, and whether to consider deploying an entire subset of your consolidation at a remote site due to overriding factors. But having this knowledge and flexibility gives you and your deployment team the capability to address a multitude of architectural differences that you may come across during your design and ongoing growth stages of your consolidated logging infrastructure. Even though there is a potentially high start-up cost, this will soon be spread across multiple systems as you add them in and have minimal design work to do to add systems, if you are successful in developing the deployment and planning templates just discussed.

One final note should be made on growth factors. As mentioned, the target is to get to the point of having a design template in order to be able to easily identify when additional resources are required as you add systems into your logging infrastructure. The importance of monitoring the operating capacity of all components of your infrastructure cannot be overstated, as experience has shown that logging architectures have a tendency to grow and grow rapidly. This growth can be in the form of increased logging from the originally installed systems just through their application growth and usage. But the other side of growth is the factor is that once administrators of remote or perimeter security service machines or components find out that they could relieve themselves of their local logging requirements, they are more than happy to start shipping someone else their logs, relieving themselves of the responsibility, although this doesn't entirely relieve them of the responsibility they have to set up their servers or security devices to send the logs and ensure the process continues. Additionally, these outlying security machines administrators are still responsible for responding to inquiries when the centralized team finds alerts or issues that need addressing that are directly related to their server, firewall, or other security component.

This is merely the physical and some degree of logical placement of these components; there is now the configuration and utilization of these components to consider, which are addressed in the next chapter. It is important to grasp an understanding of these influencing factors up to this point because now the real work starts coming into play: how to make use of the logical side of log capture, normalization, correlation, and, most important, the reporting work.

# Note

1. Link speed is the available bandwidth from your central repository out to your collector and end device. Recognize that the full stated capacity of a line may not be completely available to your system due to Quality of Service (QOS) settings that may reduce bandwidth specific to your application.

## Chapter 5

# Setting Up Correlation Rules, Putting Your Assembled Infrastructure to Work

Now that we have assembled the physical architecture, decided on what is to be collected, why it is to be collected, and identified some expectations, we're ready to install a logical configuration. In this section we dive into the configuration aspect of log consolidation as well as the decisions that need to be made in component configuration. It is the log consolidation and correlation configuration that show the value of our implementation. (You do more than just replay back the data that you have collected in its raw form.)

Some examples of how we correlate the log data include the following:

1. *Consolidation of like devices.* This approach provides a big picture of total events from one type of device across the enterprise; for example, all firewall rule denies from all external portals with a common source or destination IP address.
2. *Consolidation of disparate devices.* These devices have one or more common factors. For example, firewalls and localized router event logs that share common traffic; this is a more advanced form of data correlation.

3. *Combination of heterogeneous devices.* These devices may appear at first glance as having nothing in common whatsoever, but upon deeper analysis clearly show a common thread and benefit of looking at heterogeneous devices on a single page, for example, an enterprise Anti-Virus (AV) console that reports on virus eradications, paired with an IDS (intrusion detection system) or some other form of network- or host-based anomaly detector. This is a rather sophisticated approach that would be useful when an infected device begins spewing out bad traffic. The AV console may simultaneously or, hopefully, very closely report that it had eradicated a virus from a device in the network vicinity.

But let's not get ahead of ourselves with all the possibilities. Let's begin at square one.

For our analysis, let's assume that we've selected a group of devices from which to collect data. Let's also assume that the devices are the same, for example, four border firewalls between the enterprise and external networks. We have also identified the reason for collection and consolidation of the data into usable form. Now how do we synthesize the data into an intelligent and usable report?

Without any logical configuration, our administrators would have had to look at each firewall log individually, finding little or no correlation among them on one screen. But now we've set up an architecture that will consolidate and feed all four logs into a common repository, with a "normalization" process that is quite simplistic. (As noted, this was a very basic implementation, but even so, it wouldn't be so hard to bring in four different makes of firewalls or even two, as the log fields would most likely have a high ratio of common fields.) Table 5.1 depicts a logical format of a simple implementation.

There are a few initial steps that must be taken when deciding to combine any number of firewalls into your consolidated logging system. These basic steps are as follows:

1. Identify the devices (firewalls), including manufacturer, model, version, and network location.
2. Make a risk assessment of the data (refer to the discussion in Chapter 4 on the topic of data sensitivity).
3. Make a determination if a standard normalizer exists for the device and version you are running and from which you are planning to collect log data.
4. Identify the data path from the endpoint/firewall.

Assuming the COTS (commercial off-the-shelf) product for log consolidation handles the devices that you have selected for collection, we

**Table 5.1    Distributed Firewall Authentication Failures**

| Date | Time[a] | Firewall | Error No. | Source |
|---|---|---|---|---|
| 250404 | 5:30:01 | PIX_West | A1 | 218.45.3.12 |
| 250404 | 5:30:30 | PIX_West | A1 | 218.45.3.12 |
| 250404 | 5:31:06 | PIX_West | A1 | 218.45.3.12 |
| 250404 | 5:40:02 | Ckpt_East | A1 | 218.45.3.12 |
| 250404 | 5:40:58 | Ckpt_East | A1 | 218.45.3.12 |
| 250404 | 5:41:23 | Ckpt_East | A1 | 218.45.3.12 |
| 250404 | 5:41:59 | Ckpt_East | A1 | 218.45.3.12 |
| 250404 | 5:42:25 | Ckpt_East | A1 | 218.45.3.12 |
| 250404 | 5:42:55 | Ckpt_East | A1 | 218.45.3.12 |
| 250404 | 5:50:03 | PIX_UK | A1 | 218.45.3.12 |
| 250404 | 5:50:39 | PIX_UK | A1 | 218.45.3.12 |
| 250404 | 5:51:12 | PIX_UK | A1 | 218.45.3.12 |
| 250404 | 5:51:55 | PIX_UK | A1 | 218.45.3.12 |

[a] Normalized time to GMT

should be able to capture the complete log record in our common consolidated repository.

Now it is time to decide what to do with the data. To see what can be done with the collected data, let's go further in depth on this first example of capturing authentication failures from a set of distributed firewalls across your enterprise.

We have a large repository of security-relevant events from our perimeter firewalls in one place. The sheer number of consolidated event records alone would overwhelm any average administrator (even the bored ones). Now we're ready to put our correlation and reporting smarts to work using the collected data for the purpose of generating meaningful reports.

The key question is, what type of intelligent and usable reports can you extract from these four like devices at different perimeter points in your network?

To understand why anyone would want to correlate such information, you must understand how attacks from the perimeter have evolved and advanced in recent years. Attackers have long known they should come in under the radar of your intrusion detection and audit systems and have developed such techniques to do so. One such technique is to attack in low numbers at multiple points. In doing so, the assumption is that no one person is looking at all the device logs. Moreover, by keeping attack numbers low, a hacker will most likely evade detection and be permitted to continue a slow but methodical undetected attack for an indefinite period of time. But now that we have a tool to combine our distributed firewalls into a single consolidated device, we can combine the same attack types from all four firewalls, take an event summary total, and select a benchmark high or low on which to report. This sounds easy and actually is, if you have selected an appropriate tool and configured its collection and report capability correctly.

Taking a step further, with our firewall logs now consolidated, we want to check failed authentications (making the assumption they are all the same firewall type, or even if they are different you can identify this "like" error with some manual analysis or through the use of your normalizer). To do so, we can set a rule to search for an occurrence of a specific error code (or group of error codes), set a summation, and develop a single alert or report line with a calculated total. Last, we must decide on a number to report on; let's assume a reporting threshold of 100 failed authentication occurrences. (The reason for this last step is that you don't want to generate an alert when there is only one failed authentication occurrence. This could be a "fat-fingered" administrator, who commonly makes a mistake on his first attempt, but every time thereafter, gets in okay and is appropriately authenticated.) Sometimes the process of setting thresholds to report on is a tuning process. For example, setting a reporting threshold at 50 occurrences initially may still get a high number of hits because of daily scans that are considered normal traffic. But we still want to know if there is some sort of spike beyond normal "white noise" so we would have to set the reporting threshold at 75 or 100 occurrences to detect an abnormality.

A secondary sort that may also be useful in the reporting rule would be correlation of the source IP address to the event type. This is a useful sort assuming that the attack comes from the same attacker (although the more advanced distributed attackers come from different sources at each attack, but this isn't always true). So in actuality, both reports should be developed, where the two rules would look like:

1. SUM [Where Error Code = 'Failed Authentication'] and ALERT if SUM => 75 Where REPORT STRING = "nn Consolidated 'Failed Authentications' "
2. SUM [Where Error Code = 'Failed Authentication'] and Source IP = {SAME} and ALERT if SUM => 75 Where REPORT STRING = "nn Consolidated 'Failed Authentications' from Source IP = nn.nn.nn.nn"

The SUM and ALERT are "actions" the correlation system takes in evaluating the data, and the REPORT STRING is the output record to be written to your summarized log report. The value of this type of consolidated reporting is readily apparent because it will show when we are receiving large numbers of attempted log-ins on our perimeter firewalls. Even though the attempts are failing, and may not be individually reported on, when combined the report will show a coordinated attack on the enterprise. By adding the second rule where the source IP address is the same, it would report a clearly coordinated attack at multiple gates although in low numbers at the individual perimeter devices, but when combined indicate a coordinated attack.

The example we've used is a simple rule set used to show how consolidation of inputs can be correlated to add value. It should be recognized that this basic correlation approach has likely been overcome by average attackers, as by now they are well aware of our capabilities. So now let's look at more advanced rule sets just to keep the hackers busy and on their toes.

The next level of correlation rules relies on collecting events from disparate devices. For this example, let's look at other enterprise security alerting device(s), ones with some form of commonality with another security or vulnerability device, such that when combined we can obtain a broad picture of the security event occurring. Let's use a combination of an enterprise AV console that receives reports when a virus is eradicated on a "network-registered" machine. This is a common scenario in today's enterprise desktop antivirus implementation, along with network IDS or IPS (intrusion prevention system) devices that detect anomalous network traffic. Because both systems detect events on the internal network, and both have in common a source IP address within the network, these two devices can easily be correlated. Reporting includes not only that an anomalous event occurred, but also some IDS/IPS event by listing a possible candidate or a suspect source. It may be coincidental that an anomalous event was detected on the network near a device logging on another security tool, but if a common internal source IP address is found between anomalous network traffic and a machine with an eradicated virus, there is probably more then just a mere coincidence. This type of reporting assumes that there is a match by IP address, indicated by having such a rule written and some threshold set low, as it is unlikely that this type of match would occur on a regular basis. So the rule would look something like this:

```
1. Where Source IP of AV Log = Source IP of IDS/IPS
   log WHERE REPORT STRING = 'Anomaly Detected &
   Virus Eradicated from Source IP nn.nn.nn.nn'
```

This approach not only generates a security event report, but also takes the problem resolution down to a further detail by correlating and reporting on the source IP. It provides analysis detail (the source IP) to the forensics team, or probably in this case the security operations team, as this type of event probably doesn't warrant a full-fledged forensics investigation, but is rather an operational event alert. Nevertheless, the combination of these two sources (the antivirus log and the anomaly detection log), now provides much more value to the report than each device would individually. On a single log report, such as the antivirus report, it would show that some number of machines had a virus or Trojan code detected and eradicated (or if advanced enough to have Spyware detectors in place, they also show a detection but do not correlate it with actual malicious traffic generated by the rogue code). This shows how the tools we've used are good tools, but alone they merely perform an assigned task within their scope (and this clearly isn't enough in our ever-changing environment).

Similarly, the anomaly detection device log would show that something was "seen" on the network that could be classified as malicious or bad—but not much more. But by combining devices we can see that not only was a piece of malicious code eradicated from one of the network devices, but also that it was malicious enough that it was causing detectable "bad" traffic on the network, which is a more serious event. Again, it is obvious that the value of the sum is greater than the parts. To take this example one step further, it is recommended that this type of report should not only occur on a daily basis, but also should be developed into a trend analysis over a period of time. The reason is that if you can identify trends attributable to specific machines, then it will clearly show that certain machines are more prone to viruses or Trojan code, and that further risk mitigation steps should be taken for this type of machine(s).

Imagine a scenario where corporate laptops are operated outside the corporate environment, possibly on the road, connected to foreign networks (much more than other machines), and possibly in more hostile environments (such as a wireless LAN at a trade show or conference which abounds in rogue traffic, many times put there to show the value of various security tools being sold at the conference). Using this scenario we would likely find high numbers of specific machines repeatedly showing up on the "Virus Detected, Machine Eradicated" report. There are network tools now available that can be set up as a network gateway, such that all machines connecting through this gateway are automatically scanned at a very detailed level, and if any form of malicious code, or lack of security settings or AV software is detected, the machine is routed to a "quarantine" network so as not to expose the corporate network to the high risk of a poorly configured or infected machine(s).

If this type of scanning gateway is implemented, we can safely assume it is a good idea to incorporate its logging mechanisms and generate some automated reporting. The report should capture the machine name, and generate some form of historical reporting mechanism to tally how many times particular machines get quarantined due to nonstandard software, or detected anomalies, and this should be correlated with the AV and Spyware detection console reports. If combined status reporting of networked machines or machines entering the network identify specific machines regularly showing up on the report from one or more of the anomaly detectors, then it should be marked as highly suspect and the user should be approached to determine what usage practices are causing it to become a repeat offender. Again, thresholds should be determined and put in place, so if a single machine shows up once as correlated among your AV console, Spyware console, and the quarantined machine console, that probably does not warrant an investigation and tracking down of the owner. Some number greater than two or three occurrences should be cause for action, as the user may have inadvertently worked in an unsafe environment on a one-time basis and picked up rogue code pieces. But if the same machine does come up on all three consoles multiple times, then it is an indication that the user is computing in a highly insecure environment, or possibly performing actions that cause the machine to operate in an unsafe mode (such as disabling or purposely deleting required security software or settings).

This last point shows that we may not only be developing a better security monitoring and alerting tool, but also generating the need for additional security protection approaches because of the additional risks identified on the network. This isn't a bad thing, but it will rapidly broaden project scope as you may introduce additional security tools as a result of your findings.

As we move progressively toward a more complex correlation, it should be clear how the combining and harvesting of the data when combined add value to enterprise security tools.

This next example starts to really expand the breadth of our log collection and reporting capabilities, and also provide us with yet another view of the integrity of the security infrastructure. In this example we introduce a template that can be used to document and set up our correlations. Over time, correlating data can get quite complex and we'll need an audit trail to track development as well as intended/expected output. For simplicity the template only shows the high-level documentation of the intended correlation, although we may need to go into more programmatic detail. The goal is to have a standard approach in developing correlation planning and implementation. Table 5.2 depicts a high-level correlation planning template completed for the next example.

### Table 5.2 Correlation Planning Template

| | | |
|---|---|---|
| **Output Report Name:** | Network Access Domain Mis-Match | |
| | | |
| **Input Source #1:** | Physical Badge Access Activity | |
| **Collected Log File Name:** | Successful Access Activity Log | |
| **Collected Fields:** | | |
| **Field 1:** | Badge ID | |
| **Field 2:** | Employee Number—Badge Holder | Index Field |
| **Field 3:** | Employee Name | |
| **Field 4:** | Reader ID/Turnstile | |
| **Field 5:** | Access Date | |
| **Field 6:** | Access Time | |
| **Field 7:** | Access Direction (entry/exit) | |
| | | |
| **Input Source #2:** | RADIUS Authentication Server Log | |
| **Collected Log File Name:** | Successful Access Activity Log | |
| **Collected Fields:** | | |
| **Field 1:** | Access Date | |
| **Field 2:** | Access Time | |
| **Field 3:** | Access ID | |
| **Field 4:** | User Name | |
| **Field 5:** | Employee Number | Index Field |
| | | |
| **Input Source #3:** | Active Directory Domain ID Access | |
| **Collected Log File Name:** | ID Access | |
| Collected Fields: | | |
| **Field 1:** | Date | |
| **Field 2:** | Time | |
| **Field 3:** | UserID | |
| **Field 4:** | Employee Number | Index Field |
| **Field 5:** | Source/Workstation network ID | |
| **Field 6:** | Auth code | |
| | | |
| **Output:** | | |
| **Local Console:** | Logcon local | |
| **Message/Record Text:** | "Domain Authentication Mis-Match; UID: nnnnnn without perimeter access authentication" | |
| **Remote Console:** | Network Operations Console | |
| **Message/Record Text:** | "Domain Authentication Mis-Match; UID: nnnnnn without perimeter access authentication" | |
| **Pager Alert:** | N/A | |
| **Message/Record Text:** | | |
| **E-Mail Alert:** | N/A | |
| **Message/Record Text:** | | |

In this example we show correlation between perimeter authentications and network domain access. In theory for every network domain access record (such as an Active Directory log-in or LDAP access), there should be a corresponding perimeter access record, either in the form of a physical access, such as through a physical badge reader access, or a remote access record through the RADIUS RAS (remote access server). If a successful network domain access occurs without a corresponding perimeter access occurring (physical or logical), then a flag record should be generated indicating a possible shared domain account, or other unauthorized access.

In this example a few complexities emerge that should be understood so that in our COTS tool selection we know what capabilities are needed to be able to execute in such a correlation rule list. We would set up this report to have the inputs as listed on the Correlation Planning Template. Be aware that it's not just a matter of searching for a common field and reporting the record; there is some degree of calculations that must be performed before reporting a potential trigger for suspicious activity. Remember we're looking for cases where there is a network domain access record, without a corresponding perimeter access record (physical badge reader or remote access authentication) within a certain time span. Questions that need to be answered include:

1. How close to the domain access does the perimeter access have to occur?
2. What is a reasonable timeframe to allow for a user to badge into the building and then execute his domain log-in? Twenty minutes or two hours?
3. How much time from when a user first enters the building may elapse before the user can reasonably be expected to log on to the domain? A user could enter the building at 7:55 a.m. but go directly into a day full of meetings and not have an opportunity to log into the domain until 4:00 p.m. that afternoon. This should not be shown as a suspicious activity event trigger, as this could generate a fair amount of false positives and where just such a case may occur, and the investigation team may end up confronting senior management personnel whose work schedule fits just these criteria.

Figure 5.1 depicts the process flowchart for this type of correlation, with the key criteria not only checking for a matching perimeter authentication, but also performing a time search for a perimeter authentication record that occurred within 8.5 hours of the domain authentication and access authorization. The generation of this report of course assumes that you have collected as inputs your AD log-on records, your physical

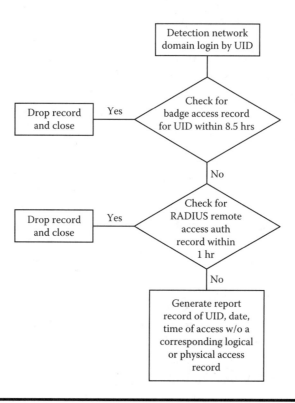

**Figure 5.1 Flowchart for network domain authentication mismatch**

badging records, and your RADIUS remote access authentication records. Collection of any one or all of these is not beyond the capabilities of these types of log consolidation systems, and, in fact, will generate a lot of value when placed in a single repository as depicted here.

Setting the time check prior to the domain log-on is required to reduce the potential for false positives as explained above. Additional field record checks would also have to occur in order to differentiate between standard user IDs and process IDs, which, of course, wouldn't have any form of recognized perimeter authentication. Only true users assigned IDs would have the perimeter authentication requirement, that is, carbon-based unit, a.k.a. human beings. The point here is that this shows the degree of rule sophistication that is required for our log consolidation tool.

Building on the emerging complexity of rule sets, and going back to the last example, let's explore the reality of how monitoring tools can be further used to protect the network. In the last example, we showed alerts generated from our reports as a "suspected" mismatch between network domain log-on and perimeter authentication within a "reasonable" period of time. But what if there were enough confidence built up that these mismatches were indeed unauthorized accesses to the domain, and hence should not have been permitted to occur in the first place? Can the log consolidation and reporting tool be configured to exert specific privileged commands that terminate the more than suspected authorized domain log-on attempts? This question illustrates the very basis of the emerging intrusion prevention systems technology, which states that there is enough confidence that certain clearly identified anomalous traffic should be stopped, not just detected. If we have enough confidence in the alerts generated by our log consolidation, the SEM (Security Event Management) tool, and the corresponding rule sets, then why not act on this information rather then merely generate alert reports and expend human resources on investigation and resolution efforts?

We may have now turned our passive logging tool into a proactive or rather reactive security tool that affects operations, hopefully only in a positive manner that provides further protections over the network infrastructure, but also requires a much higher degree of confidence gained through benchmarking reporting, rules, and thresholds. Without conducting this benchmarking, you could be subjecting your environment to the "HAL Syndrome," this being a product of *2001: A Space Odyssey*, where HAL (referred to as the Heuristic ALgorithm, the ship's master computer) takes over complete system control without human intervention. In the movie, "Dave" was locked out in deep space pleading with HAL to "Open the bay doors, HAL," and HAL resisted as Dave was considered a threat to the system. If we leave too much of the automated decision making up to the system, it may have unforeseen circumstances not thought out or discovered during the "burn-in" phase, and with little human intervention these automated responses may occur faster than we can control. Not that the author is completely against such automated response, but just one that warrants extensive testing and validation before implementing, as well as a human override system to reverse any silicon-based automated decision making.

One method to reduce the false positives that could lead to unwanted automated responses, or false log reports is commonly referred to as "tuning the process," and we should look at some of the nuances of the effort. We cannot overstate the importance of tuning the process in order to ensure as few false positives as possible, especially if we do incorporate some degree of an automated response or automated prevention mechanism, and the system is programmed to act on it.

Rarely is a correlation rule written just once that generates meaningful report data on the first go-round. There is always some form of tuning required. The simplest tuning is done on a threshold number of events where an alert report is generated only when a significant number of events occur, not on every single event. Going back to the first example of log consolidation of four perimeter firewalls, the tuning was performed to select some threshold number of events required before reporting a "failed log-on attempt" on any one of the perimeter firewalls. The objective was to only report significant events, worthy of attention or follow-up and resolution. Now let's return our tuning exercise to the previous correlation example, *Network Domain Log-In Mismatches.*

In this example, we want to report on any recorded domain log-ins from a standard user ID that did not have a corresponding perimeter access record (physical or logical, badge reader, or Remote Access Server authentication record). We recognize that there may be a time gap between the time the perimeter authentication occurred, and when the actual network domain log-in occurred, so we analyzed this out to 8.5 hours. But after running this report rule set for a period of time, we find that we have a large number of alerts, and upon further investigation find that users were authorized, as the company has a large number of the workforce on a 4 × 10 work week (4 days at 10 hours each day). If these users also had full-day meetings scheduled, which kept them from their desks for the first 8 to 8.5 hours, then they would obviously show up on our report. This is where the tuning process comes into play. It is not an immediate task; it is a task that must be analyzed over time. Therefore, the rule set may initially go into place with an 8.5 hour threshold, then based on verified false positives (i.e., authorized log-ins that were originally flagged), then the rule would have to be adjusted to no longer report these false positives (the 4 × 10 workers), and only report actual cases of unauthorized access by extending the time span from 8.5 hours out to possibly 9.5 hours or more.

Additional tuning may also be required to enhance security thresholds, but this will take even more analysis. Still using the Network Domain Log-In Mismatch example, the following question emerges. Should there be a different time span variable for users entering the network via RAS (either via dial-up or VPN) than for those physically on site coming in via the badge reader? This is a debatable question, based on the complexity of the network. One train of thought states that once a user accesses the network via RAS, she should next execute a Network Domain Log-In. Idle time spent at the domain prompt should be considered suspect and potentially alerted. This is true in a pure Windows domain environment, as there is nowhere else for the user to go once they pass the RAS log-in. However, in a heterogeneous network, with non-AD domain-based UNIX environments, perceived idle time may actually be their UNIX environment log-in which then wouldn't be registered in the Active Directory network domain log-in. (The latter UNIX example shouldn't be identified as a mismatch because RAS access to a UNIX environment should be allowed.) This is why the mismatch report only gets triggered starting with an AD Network Domain Log-In record as the process flow in Figure 5.3 depicts.

Another example of complex rules and the power of correlation that should be covered and that goes further into the realm of "what if" scenarios is the Internet Gateway URL Blocking (IGB) tool. (If IP appears on the URL filter denied list, antivirus eradication report, then IP = record on the Suspicious Machine list.) This example brings in the logs from a tool which is becoming very common in enterprise environments. Internet Gateway Blocking comes with predefined policies set up to block access from a corporate enterprise environment to potentially harmful Web sites on the Internet. Such categories may include hacking sites, anonymizers, WARZ downloads (illegal software copy downloads), gambling, and other potentially harmful or otherwise "inappropriate" Web sites for a corporate customer to be visiting during work hours, or for that matter anytime from the corporate environment.

The IGB tool maintains various activity logs. One particularly informative report shows machines that were denied outbound access because of attempts to access a specified prohibited site or group of sites in a banned category. Of course the logs provided by the tool can themselves supply sorting and high water marks (i.e., hitting predefined numbers of events in a given period of time) or threshold reports, but inasmuch as we are in the consolidation mode, let's combine the IGB logs with one of our other report sets, such as the combination of our AV console, Spyware console, and maybe even our anomalous traffic detector (although the latter may not be as valuable in this combination for the reasons to follow). Now we find some commonality where a virus-eradicated machine was found to be trying to communicate back to a "bad site" possibly flagged as part of the hacker community, because the Trojan program it caught was programmed to "phone home."

The anomalous traffic detector may not have reported on this action because the machine was merely sending a mail message which may or may not leave a bad signature. But due to the fact that it was directed at a site that may be in the "blocked" list, the combination would put it on the highly suspect list by combining the logs from these various alerting tools. And yes, the threshold discussion also comes into play and will require tuning, even though preliminary analysis may indicate that this threshold should be set fairly low, as the prohibited sites list is fairly comprehensive and accurate. Therefore any machine found attempting to visit prohibited sites and found to have continuous or repeated AV or Spyware detection, is an indicator of more than a coincidental occurrence. In Chapter 6 we talk more about reporting of these types of events and some degree of escalation process. This is somewhat outside the scope of our discussion, but should be touched upon as there is little use in generating valuable reports on high-risk machines or users if the results are not followed up on and corrective action taken.

The foregoing examples highlight the need to have a very configurable rules engine, with the flexibility to not only write complex rule sets, but also to modify the rules with ease and reimplement the updated rule sets without great impact on the system. In the tuning process there may be multiple changes to multiple rules in order to get meaningful output (striving for a minimum number of false positives).

Another aspect of tuning is even more complex because tuning a consolidated reporting system involves more than just changing variable values (time spans, count thresholds, etc.). It may also involve taking additional actions along the lines of "IF–THEN" statements. We touched on this topic in our discussion of Network Domain Log-In Mismatch report features. The next level of tuning expands on the "THEN" portion of the rule by taking an action in respect to conducting further record correlation.

Working from our second correlation example where we correlated the antivirus eradication console log and the anomalous traffic detection log, we generated a report where there was a single common source IP identified between these two reports. Using our Correlation Planning Template, we should define an extension of this report with a third input that can only be enabled once the report has been running for a period of time. Completing the template for this new report appears as Table 5.3, Correlation Planning Template for AV and Anomaly Detection Trending.

The purpose of this report is not only to identify those machines that were potentially infected and cleaned (but not before possibly unleashing anomalous traffic onto the network, which was detected and logged by IDS or IPS devices), but also to create a trend analysis to determine if those machines were previously found to be in the same condition. This can be accomplished by running the first rule set (which identified the virus-eradicated machine and anomalous traffic, as well as generated a historical report of events to determine if the most recently detected IP had appeared in previous reports). We would then have the condition of the machine(s) with a greater degree of urgency because it is now considered a repeat offender and additional protections should now be considered. The point here is that using the original report to generate and store its output reports in a manner that can be referenced by a follow-on rule makes the system more intelligent. Your rule base can use previously generated reports that set trends, as input to a follow-on report.

Tuning a report can take on a life of its own, as well as build on itself as evidenced by the prior example. The author emphasizes the need for a highly flexible and capable toolset that allows these types of reporting rules to be written. We have now outlined a somewhat more advanced reporting process; both the run of the AV and anomaly detection report

**Table 5.3   Correlation Planning Template for AV & Anomaly Detection Trending**

| | |
|---|---|
| **Output Report Name:** | Correlation Planning Template for AV & Anomaly Detection Trending Report |
| | |
| **Input Source #1:** | Enterprise Anti-Virus Console |
| **Collected Log File Name:** | Detected Eradications @ workstation |
| **Collected Fields:** | |
| **Field 1:** | Workstation ID/name |
| **Field 2:** | Workstation IP                                    Index Field |
| **Field 3:** | Eradication Date |
| **Field 4:** | Eradication Time |
| **Field 5:** | Eradication Type (worm, trojan, virus) |
| **Field 6:** | Error Code |
| Field 7: | |
| | |
| **Input Source #2:** | Anomaly Detection Device |
| **Collected Log File Name:** | Anomaly Detecton Log—Active Detections |
| **Collected Fields:** | |
| **Field 1:** | Detect Date (Local) |
| **Field 2:** | Detect Time (local) |
| **Field 3:** | Detect Message Text |
| **Field 4:** | Source IP—as applicable/available         Index Field |
| **Field 5:** | Destination IP—as applicable/available |
| | |
| **Reference Source #3:** | Archive of AV & Anomaly Detection |
| **Input Log File Name:** | AV & Anomalies Detected File log |
| **Collected Fields:** | |
| **Field 1:** | Date |
| **Field 2:** | Time |
| **Field 3:** | Source IP |
| **Field 4:** | Anomaly Text                                        Index Field |
| **Field 5:** | |
| **Field 6:** | |
| | |
| **Output:** | |
| **Local Console:** | Logcon local |
| **Message/Record Text:** | "AV Eradication & Anomaly detected from IP nn.nn.nn.nn X times in past Y days" |
| **Remote Console:** | Network Operations Console |
| **Message/Record Text:** | "AV Eradication & Anomaly detected from IP nn.nn.nn.nn X times in past Y days" |
| **Pager Alert:** | N/A |
| **Message/Record Text:** | N/A |
| **E-Mail Alert:** | N/A |
| **Message/Record Text:** | N/A |

**Table 5.3   Correlation Planning Template for AV & Anomaly Detection Trending (continued)**

| Log Report: | Correlation Planning Template for AV & Anomaly Detection Trending Report |
|---|---|
| Log Record: | "AV Eradication & Anomaly detected from IP nn.nn.nn.nn" X times in past Y days" |

(which now creates the trending report for repeat offenders), and the use of the report for future runs, make it a supplemental input report to generate a more valuable output report.

To continue with our correlation example and how they further the security monitoring by your Security Operations Center (SOC), we should look at how the reports generated can identify an emerging threat to our enterprise environments. This threat is coming in the form of a "Zero Day" threat that will be appearing in the form of malicious attacks utilizing a recently discovered vulnerability. In the past when systems or device vulnerabilities were discovered and announced, it was usually some period of time before an actual attack surfaced. But this timeframe between vulnerability discovery and exploits showing up has been steadily decreasing thus making systems and networks more vulnerable in a shorter period of time.

Legacy intrusion detection systems relied on signature-based defense mechanisms, which had a lag time among the discovery of a vulnerability, the emergence of the exploit, and then finally the release of a detection signature. The IDS tools have since progressed beyond mere signature-based detection, moving to behavioral-based systems, which, in theory, should be able to detect threats early on, without the need of a predefined signature. The designs of these are targeted to address the dreaded Zero Day attack, though even these behavioral-based systems could use some support to shore up their ability to detect brand new attacks or exploits on their first day of release. This is where your correlation and reporting engine can come into play and possibly provide further inputs to your overall monitoring system.

Understanding how an attack starts, with some release of malicious code either launched from outside your environment or introduced inside your network, will most likely cause some number of indicators to go off within your infrastructure. The use of your collection of logs and correlation among your various detectors could be leveraged to provide an even better early warning system.

Let's look at what we should or would collect from across our enterprise in order to build such an early warning system.

We've talked of collecting from our firewalls, which is an obvious first choice, but other security systems such as your network IDS tools, antivirus enterprise console, vulnerability scanner, and now possibly even your performance-monitoring systems and trouble-ticket systems could be candidates to include in your consolidated logging architecture. This now introduces a whole new class of device into our security log consolidation system, performance-monitoring systems, and trouble-ticket systems. But as we work through this scenario, the value of these additional inputs soon becomes evident. Because this correlation rule is targeted at detecting the Zero Day threat, we are essentially chasing something we have little or no knowledge of and thus no attack signatures to feed into our standard security detection systems. Our primary reliance is on our behavioral-based systems which we hope are sophisticated enough to provide some degree of insight into this wholly unknown attack.

The value may start to emerge when we combine the detection and alerts from this disparate group of resources, in search for a common thread in their alarms to develop a single accurate alert message.

The alerts or log records will come at varying rates, but if some form of malicious code is executing within or against your environment, the expectation is that one or more of your systems will detect some degree of anomalies, though individually there may not be enough of a blip on your screens to raise attention.

So now we need to evaluate what we should try to correlate among these inputs to make our early warning system potentially effective.

Starting with our firewalls, we may see an increase in unknown denies or just an increase in general policy violations. If we are dealing with a case of an internal threat, then we would have a record of the source address of the code launch (potentially an infected machine, with a virus or Malware not yet identified or eradicated) and the possible denied message on the firewall. So we now may have a common thread, the source IP address, though not much more data, other then a slightly elevated rate of policy denies on a firewall. The next device used to interrogate the logs may be your IDSs to determine if they detected any anomalous traffic, possibly not yet defined as a hard attack, but maybe just as an anomaly. Still no definitive answer may be readily apparent, but there may be other triggers detected in each of these systems, which by themselves wouldn't warrant a red flag, but if each is a percentage point above normal, or the IP is even being logged as an anomaly, we may now begin to see a pattern.

We next may look to our performance-monitoring systems that analyze traffic patterns on your network to keep the network within optimal traffic levels. If an elevated amount of traffic is occurring on the network, these systems may alert the NOC of such changes. If minimal inputs from this system are also available to your logging or reporting tool, it may be yet another trigger. Why would a single device suddenly show up as firing

**Table 5.4   Early Warning Alert Matrix**

| IP Address—<br>Internal Machines | Firewall Deny | IDS<br>Anomaly—Undefined | Vulnerability Scanner | Performance<br>Monitoring Sys | Workstation<br>Trouble Ticket | |
|---|---|---|---|---|---|---|
| 10.94.3.10 | N | N | N | Y | Y | |
| 10.94.10.5 | Y | Y | Y | Y | Y | <- Console Alert |
| 10.72.5.3 | Y | Y | N | N | N | |
| 10.72.6.7 | Y | N | N | N | Y | |

off abnormal amounts of traffic? A final system that could be utilized is the desktop/server trouble-ticket reporting system. If minimal inputs are taken from this system, as the ticket number, date, time, and device ID in the form of an IP address, this could be yet another trigger point that could be utilized to map suspicious activity.

If we found that our suspicious internal IP address, which has been showing up listed on the other systems, has also been reported as having some form of a problem, then this could be the final trigger that would warrant firing off a console alert message against this device, with an indicator of the triggers that caused this alert. Table 5.4 outlines a short decision matrix that would be part of the programmed decision process whether to fire off a console message if all these triggers were positive for a given IP address.

Note that there are several different IPs that show up on this matrix as having been detected by one or more of these inputs. Only one IP shows up on all of these devices, the 10.94.10.5, as it had an entry in each of the console logs of the systems indicated. The other IP addresses may have had an entry on some of the other devices, but none across the board. The final decision maker would be that our most suspect address also had a trouble-ticket system entry, so there was clearly a reported problem with this device. Additionally, one may note why other reports may not have detected this single IP independently because it obviously does have a log entry in one or more security systems. The point is that the number of entries for that IP address in any one of these systems may be well below the thresholds of your reports; hence, it would not show up on any of your "normal" summarized log reports.

A final note should be made regarding the inclusion of nonsecurity-specific devices in your infrastructure. Because these are not core security tools, you may not be required to preserve these log records, as you are only using them as supplements to your security monitoring and alerting function. Therefore, you may not have the retention cycles that you do for the rest of your systems, and may be able to keep these records only for very short periods of time, thus not overburdening your system whose focus is on utilizing and preserving security log information.

So far we've looked at correlation rules purely from an end-device perspective (or bottom-up requirements), based on consolidating logs from two or more security-related devices. But there is also an approach that sometimes drives consolidation efforts that comes from the "top down." In this approach a problem is identified and a solution set must be found using existing tools or acquiring additional tools specifically for the problem. Top-down reporting requirements may come in the form of an assurance report, where the report is required on a periodic basis and which requires proof or evidence of integrity or controls within the enterprise.

These requirements would come in the form of emerging regulatory actions. One such example is the explosive growth of regulatory issues in the world of information technology and industry-specific requirements. New regulations such as Gramm–Leach–Bliley, Sarbanes–Oxley, and California's SB1386 and AB1950 all require system controls, protections, and the ability to verify or prove the existence of said controls. Under these regulations, the security professional is required to prove that adequate security controls are in place. The question must be asked whether the tools are already in place to meet these regulatory demands or if additional tools are required.

With this new requirement in front of us, we must go back to our palette of security tools to determine if we can meet these and pass the test. Some of the audit logs that we are collecting provide some degree of proof that we are actively monitoring the network; these can be used as evidence of controls being in place. Some SEM vendors are now providing templates specifically for the regulations, outlining what should be collected, event and logwise, and including static reports designed to address the requirement. For installation of any log consolidation/SEM tool, it is highly recommended to raise awareness of applicable regulations, and how the tools can be used to meet said requirements. Moving forward, we use a top-down approach (versus where we started previously from a bottom-up approach) for the development of our infrastructure and rule base for correlation and reporting. In the next chapter we go into more depth on the reporting structure and into the alerting aspect of your consolidating logging architecture.

## Chapter 6

# Security Event Management, Generating Reports from Your System

Thus far, we have built a highly scalable distributed heterogeneous log consolidation and correlation architecture, based on a commercial off-the-shelf (COTS) product with a strong and flexible rules engine. Examples of how to apply these rules were demonstrated in Chapter 5. In this section we dig deeper into the reporting aspect of log consolidation Security Incident Manager (SIM) and Security Event Manager (SEM) infrastructure. We also look at the benefits of focusing on event reporting and differentiate "alerting" from active logging and security event reporting. The combination of these features makes up the overall management aspect of SIM/SEM and SAM (Security Alert Manager).

As we delve into this topic, we see a multitude of security reporting opportunities emerge. In addition, as we begin to understand the depth of our internal reporting capabilities, we are able to provide external reporting. But be careful, as the user community becomes aware of reporting capabilities, the demand for reporting will become greater as will the demand for various formats and media increase. Some reporting examples we look at include (but are not limited to) alerting consoles at the NOC (Network Operations Center) and SOC (Security Operations Center), Web delivery (for ad hoc access), key individuals, and even mobile devices.[1]

Another aspect of network security alerts that emerges as a result of our reporting is the "escalation method." This is a very important aspect of the entire security viewpoint of the game, but should not be confused with the logging and SOC reporting aspect. In the next chapter we go into more depth on the escalation process, which of course follows the overall reporting process; it provides a process of "what to do" once you have the report.

## Security Event and Incident Management and Reporting

So now we have a centralized architecture acting as the primary repository and collection point for security-relevant events from a multitude of devices and tools. We also have written rule sets that allow us to gain value from these devices showing that the combination of events can provide higher value when reported in a refined manner. (This is all based on the intelligence built into the rule sets such that they reflect experience in detecting security-relevant events or incidents based on the combination of existing tools and what they detect in one manner or another.) Let's now go in-depth on the reporting aspect of the high-value data that was extracted from our security devices and get prepared to generate a broad array of reports.

We have a multitude of events being reported; some areas are more security-relevant than others, all have some type of value, some require priority attention, whereas others are follow-up, and others are merely informational for now (we speak further on classification of events and reports in Chapter 7).

The first reporting methodology is for the security operations center. Alerts generated for the SOC are reported in the form of a console text message (which is also archived to a console SOC log). In the SOC we assume there is a high degree of subject matter experts and that this staff has the analytical capability to review the information and perform intelligent analysis of the reports or suspected security incident. In addition, because our system was designed with thresholds in mind, SOC personnel shouldn't be overwhelmed with streams of false positives, but will only be alerted by events once they become or are near critical.

We saw examples of console text messages in the correlation section. Development of both a console text message and an archived report is necessary depending on the functional reporting structure of the enterprise. Do we have a full-time 7 × 24 functional SOC staff receiving regular console messages with the ability to quickly react? Or do we have partial SOC coverage that pulls periodic reports for review and analysis after the fact with a delayed reaction to potential security events? In order to offer

**Table 6.1    Firewall Authentication Failures—Detailed Records**

| Date | Time[a] | Firewall | Error No. | Source |
|------|------|----------|-----------|--------|
| 250404 | 5:30:01 | PIX_West | A1 | 218.45.3.12 |
| 250404 | 5:30:30 | PIX_West | A1 | 218.45.3.12 |
| 250404 | 5:31:06 | PIX_West | A1 | 218.45.3.12 |
| 250404 | 5:40:02 | Ckpt_East | A1 | 218.45.3.12 |
| 250404 | 5:40:58 | Ckpt_East | A1 | 218.45.3.12 |
| 250404 | 5:41:23 | Ckpt_East | A1 | 218.45.3.12 |
| 250404 | 5:41:59 | Ckpt_East | A1 | 218.45.3.12 |
| 250404 | 5:42:25 | Ckpt_East | A1 | 218.45.3.12 |
| 250404 | 5:42:55 | Ckpt_East | A1 | 218.45.3.12 |
| 250404 | 5:50:03 | PIX_UK | A1 | 218.45.3.12 |
| 250404 | 5:50:39 | PIX_UK | A1 | 218.45.3.12 |
| 250404 | 5:51:12 | PIX_UK | A1 | 218.45.3.12 |
| 250404 | 5:51:55 | PIX_UK | A1 | 218.45.3.12 |

[a] Normalized time to GMT

the maximum report flexibility, our reporting design should be capable of supporting both current and after-the-fact reporting.

Working from our early sample report that showed a correlation between four different firewalls with detected authentication failures, one of our report strings was:

```
nn Consolidated 'Failed Authentications'
```

With many of the COTS SEM tools available, console messages that are directed to SOC personnel provide the ability to drill down to the source data that triggered the alert. Now recall that the alert was based upon a predefined number of log-in attempts to multiple perimeter firewalls in the enterprise (which should be configured to have a high degree of scrutiny). By clicking on the report string, the analyst can access a greater detail of the records that generated the event. Table 6.1 illustrates drill-down data executed from a console message.

From this example we see that the alert data detail is "behind" the console message sent to the SOC and available via this drill-down methodology. The ability to access this message detail should be available only to limited system users, your SOC analysts, as this data could be deemed sensitive and is not something that you want to advertise to the world or beyond your most trusted personnel. A further reason to limit this group is due to the impact on the system that this drill process may cause, as it is performing in-depth queries to the core data repository. The opportunity and availability for near real-time queries require that the system quickly be optimized to service anticipated requests. The downside to this action is that drill-down to full database queries will have a direct impact on the back-end system.

So, the issue becomes our ability to offer drill-down capability from a SOC console message, while at the same time minimizing the impact on the overall system. As we strategize to minimize system impact from drill-down tasks, it would be wise to assume a reduced performance of concurrent console usage by 10 to 20 percent.[2] One of the first things that can be done to minimize system impact is to limit drill-down capabilities to a defined group of users. The decision to limit usage of the drill-down capability is crucial to maintaining system performance as this type of usage and the performance hit against the database can have a huge impact on the entire system. When a query is initiated, potentially the entire database takes the hit. We must be aware that a query will result whenever SOC staff decides to drill down from a console message. It is important to emphasize that drill-down capability should only be given to those who really need it and can provide a measurable benefit to the enterprise.

So we've got some potential issues with system performance; let's also have a look at the alternatives. One option is the generation of subsidiary reports under existing high-level alerts such that the key data is reported in batch mode and made available to the users who receive the reports (even though they don't have the immediate need for the detailed records of each alert). The result is a static report that can be followed up with a "point in time" drill-down report available with a single click of the mouse to a batch-generated report for the previous 24 or 48 hours. This type of capability removes the requirement to give real-time drill-down capabilities to more people than is necessary but still provides for an additional level of detail as requested or required.

The output would be similar to Figure 6.1, but just not in real-time. It would be delivered as a link in e-mail or an e-mail link contained in a stored report on a Web page (best linked via SSL to provide a level of encryption). The tricky part is calculating the required degree of "currency" for the report: 48 hours may be too long so 24 hours is a good minimum. The batch report should be generated during the time of least processing on the system during the previous 24 hours. This would then provide a degree of current detail (assuming the recipient has a need on a daily basis to review this level of detail), and yet it doesn't put too great a

Network operations center consoles

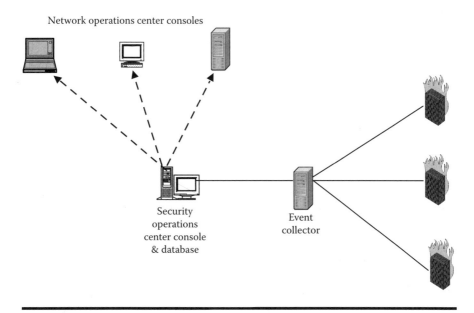

Security operations center console & database

Event collector

**Figure 6.1    Log collection to alert generation**

burden on the system. The output will look something like Figure 6.1, Detailed Records, the result of a drill-down, but would contain many more records as it would also include all activity from the previous 24 hours.

A few examples of this type of batch reporting may be the Failed Authentication report as indicated, but with more records because it covers a long span of time. Other such reports could be the correlation report between your enterprise virus console and your IDS (intrusion detection system), whereby it produces a batch report identifying segments where signatures of malicious code were detected and segments where desktop virus eradications had occurred based on your enterprise virus console report. The benefit of this batch reporting is that this can be a key threat mitigation report by providing the status of your enterprise and not requiring the subject matter experts to be constantly keeping watch. The report can contain the detail down to the machines detected by the IDS, and the machines that had eradications occur from the virus consoles, all combined on the one report. The batch process of generating it also minimizes the real-time impact on the system during prime operating hours.

As we look at batch reporting, we should also think about external batch reporting options that provide additional opportunities to maximize our reporting capability. As previously mentioned there are other organizations within the enterprise that can benefit from the source data that we now have the ability to correlate (and we should take advantage of this opportunity because rarely do security organizations have the opportunity to be a service to the organization versus a perceived burden to it!). This is an opportunity to promote our security organization through our ability to provide value reporting outside the security group. As we move further into this topic, we must keep in mind that it is not the charter of SOC staff to provide external reporting. But the question remains: why not leverage the security group's ability to provide external report value via its system reporting without adversely affecting system performance. Knowing that external customers who receive these batch reports don't require the same level of detail or timeliness of reports that SOC and NOC personnel require, the challenge is to be able to generate a meaningful and detailed report to the customer within a usable timeframe without overextending security resources.

Batch file reports should all deliver some degree of detail. They should look much like what the real-time SOC staff sees, albeit received via batch process at predefined periodic intervals. In addition, given that it is for external user groups, it must be relevant enough to be of value. If there is a need for more detailed and current information, then a request can be referred to the SOC call number for further analysis and assistance.

The batch report should have a run cap on it for size, possibly only showing the top 'nn' number of events, or past 'n' number of hours so that it doesn't get too large under extreme circumstances. It should also have a set retention period (knowing the original records are preserved, this is merely a forwarded report and, therefore, the report itself wouldn't have any set retention requirements). The only question here is how long the end users require the ability to view these reports. Given the fact that it is a drill-down, with detailed reporting, and probably only periodically utilized, a short retention period is recommended, possibly as short as a week. This will all be decided as a result of the user community, and more important, experience and trials of the reporting infrastructure. A few additional considerations for retention include the size of the reports and storage capacities. Are the reports stored on a single central server or distributed across your enterprise? A distributed approach spreads the storage load out among multiple servers, possibly making better use of resources, but also introduces additional risk of distributing security reports. This could also potentially mean added costs to protect these reports. If the reports are distributed to outlying hosting servers and it were deemed necessary to encrypt the reports, then multiple SSL encryption keys would have to be purchased, at least one for each distributed host server receiving and redistributing the security reports. In some cases if the central server were sized appropriately, economies of scale in storage could make the centralized approach more cost effective.

An example of an external group that could benefit outside your core security group is your network operations group. The fact that you could be collecting from a multitude of devices, but most important, your firewalls, both on the perimeter and internally, you will have near real-time data from these devices at a single point from across your enterprise. This may cross product boundaries as well, such as between your Checkpoint and Cisco Pix firewalls; the point here is each of these has its own management console, but it is specific to its own product arena. You have the benefit of being able to collect from both and view them side by side on a single console. Generating reports of firewall denies and overall activity (from a security perspective) can be quite helpful to the network group by showing possible misconfiguration of other network devices or components, especially those facing the internal firewalls. If a firewall is suddenly denying a high volume of traffic and it generates identifying records where this traffic is coming from, this could be quite useful to the network performance management group. Events such as this may go undetected by their normal network sensors (until they reach a critical mass), but your ongoing reporting structure may provide an early warning type of alert across a heterogeneous platform of devices. (In fact, it has been the author's experience that the network group not only wants to see such reports, but has gone to the point of requesting real-time console access to make its own queries once it was discovered that all the log data was available in a single console access.)

This discussion further makes the case for plenty of advance planning of the overall system needs prior to diving into a purchase. By having the whole architecture laid out in advance, including the aspect of reporting cycle, it will help in making cost-effective purchases based on estimated sizing of components such as mass storage, server encryption, user base, and systems to be managed.

A final consideration for generating any number of static reports is protection and access controls. Because the reports are static implies that they will be stored somewhere for some period of time and this scenario creates a risk factor. If the reports were deemed valuable and included information from a multitude of security systems, they would therefore warrant adequate protection. Protections available depend on the methodology utilized to generate the batch reports. Many SEM products today have protection capabilities for the reasons stated previously (relieving the system of volumes of real-time ad hoc queries against the main data repository). Because the COTS products have built-in scheduled report generation capabilities, some may also include protected output queues. These are usually built around some form of role-based access control. This gives the report providers the ability to grant report access by user group or role-based access. In the best-case scenario, the system would

**Table 6.2   Role-Based Access Controls**

| Role | OU (Organizational Unit) | Access within Reporting System |
|------|--------------------------|--------------------------------|
| ADMIN | IT | Read All, Console, online queries, batch reports |
| Manager | IT | Read All, batch reports |
| NOC Staff | IT | Read All, Console Read only, batch reports |
| Manager | Western Region | Read Selected (Regional), Batch Reports (Selected) |
| ADMIN | Western Region | Read Selected (Regional), Console Selected Batch Reports (Selected) |

use enterprise access controls, such as an LDAP directory of users, potentially even using predefined user roles. By leveraging a preexisting repository of users, logging and report administrators would not have to enter all the users into yet another directory system, with a different set of access controls and rules. Depending on the degree of roles defined in the user directory, we may be able to grant access based on the existing roles in the manner depicted in Table 6.2.

Using this sample of roles and access rights list, it could be used to grant access (and protections) over potentially sensitive data as well as system functions. Note how the IT ADMINs are the only ones with broad-based access not only to the reports but also the functions of the system such as uninhibited console access. The IT managers are merely granted Read and Batch Report access (recall how we stated that the ad hoc query function on the console must be severely restricted in order to preserve system performance). Then by further using roles such as "Regional" access, we can further restrict access not only to functions, but selected data within the reporting functions, specifically those related only to their region or area of the company. This could be identified by keying off the actual data itself, such as some identifier for a North American firewall log versus a European firewall log, either through the naming of the device or the designated IP ranges of addresses assigned to the various regions. If you are able to make this designation, then you could restrict the North American users to view only data associated with their device logs within their geographic region.

Our assumptions for applying these access controls rely on a couple of conditions: first, the COTS SEM product that was selected has the capability to base its access rights on an external LDAP directory and second, our LDAP directory has the same degree of "identity" (as in our sample) tied to each of the user entries. The first condition is not uncommon;

the issue of separate user access rights lists has always been around; in addition, the linking to the common LDAP directory of users is a logical solution set that has become quite common. The second condition may be slightly more difficult as it relies on the directory of users having the required information to be able to run a role-based access control methodology. Hopefully this won't be as challenging as having a directory that has user groups, as well as their placement within the company by OU (Organizational Unit) which is also a fairly common concept. Again, this all takes up-front knowledge and planning, especially when selecting a SEM system to know to ask questions such as, "Does the security event manager allow role-based access control from an external directory structure?"

We've begun to cover basic reporting from SOC real-time to nonrealtime batch NOC reports delivered to non-SOC personnel. Let's dig deeper into external reporting options.

Let's start with one of our previous external reporting scenarios, where we reported on suspicious desktop machines that were identified in reports when correlated with eradicated viruses and potential sources of suspicious network traffic. The report of course has security ramifications, but it may also be useful to desktop support personnel whose responsibility it is to ensure that current desktop protection software is deployed, or if a deployment effort or update failed, which led to the desktop (or groups of desktops) showing up on the SOC alert report. The appropriate report for this group would be generated in batch mode (and if possible in a further attempt to maintain the efficient performance of your system), only run on the 72- to 120-hour basis (three to five days).

The recipients would be the desktop support group responsible for the timely distribution of the AV updates, as well as the base AV software. The fewer times a day or week that even batch reports are run, the better off the overall performance of this system. Our desktop support team is a good example where the data is not so time critical (infected machines that have been corrected, knowing that is one of the input sources from the enterprise virus defense system that is reporting those machines it has patched) as to not demand frequent reporting. So it soon becomes evident that this is a report that doesn't require as timely a reporting cycle, so the "Infected machine, anomalous traffic" report could be batch run on a 72-hour cycle and reported and still provide a degree of value to the end user(s). It will show those machines that had viruses detected as well as (through correlation with the network IDS) show a match to that machine as generating suspicious traffic.

If a pattern of the same machine or machines shows up on this report, analysis should be performed on that particular machine (or groups of machines) to determine if the update process is still working, or if it requires further degrees of protection because it continues to get infected and get eradications on a regular basis. Whereas other reports (i.e., firewall failed authentications) may be more sensitive and subject to the security access controls, this type of report may not be as sensitive as some of the other batch reports that we spoke of earlier, and thus they might be able to be hosted on distributed servers, not requiring encryption or, for that matter, much in the way of access control. This follows the old rule of applying security controls such that they are commensurate with the sensitivity of the data. As we continue to work through various options, we must always keep in mind the importance of delivering the data and reports in a timely manner, while still providing adequate protection to the data contained in the report.

## Security Alert Management (SAM)

SAM is also a key component of an enterprise security program; this is the alerting mechanism of any one of your security tools. It is often distributed on a product-by-product basis where each security tool has its own console and alerting mechanism. The relationship of SAM to log consolidation efforts is that your consolidated log collection contains all the SAM alerts located within it and thus provides us with a prime opportunity to also fire off alerts on a near-real-time basis (there are usually plenty of specific consoles for this purpose), but, if we are already collecting data from the multiple security devices, then it might make sense to leverage the system to generate additional near-real-time alerts to benefit the watchful eyes of SOC or NOC (although we initially focus on the NOC alerts). We are going to some depth of the concept of using your log consolidation system to create or supplement your security alert management infrastructure based on the log consolidation architecture that you are building. In Chapter 7 we go further by detailing the escalation process that should be developed to standardize how to address each of the alert types, but for now we just go into the basis of generating the alerts.

Let's begin our discussion with the basics of what can be done based on our firewall log collection system. Figure 6.1 illustrates ·a basic data flow of our log collection system and then depicts how near-real-time alerts could be relayed to the NOC console infrastructure.

On the right are the various firewalls from which data is being collected; these firewalls are feeding the intermediary log collection device, referred to as an "Event Collector." From the Event Collector, the data is passed to the main database collection point, with the master SOC console attached. At the SOC console, security alert messages are first displayed. The SOC console is normally staffed by security personnel; it may not be a physical console but a logically accessible (via a secure communication link) console. Because the SOC console is accessed only by a limited number of people, it may not be under constant watch and monitoring. Therefore, an additional set of eyes watching for key events would be very useful and practical. At this point, it makes sense to also formulate an alert architecture involving the network operations console.

Getting started on this task, we are already familiar with the "rules" that can be written to generate alerts; we also know that we can filter the data coming in and generate responses, just as we have described for the SOC console. Now we must determine what type of alerts are important enough to pass on to the NOC console and when should they be passed. We want to ensure that the alerts are relevant and not duplicates already received as part of normal NOC alerting, for example, a "firewall failover" message, which indicates when, between a pair of firewalls, one goes down and "fails over" to its backup unit. This event would likely be reported in the backup firewall log that had picked it up after the failover. This is clearly a relevant event that should be reported on, and should also be alerted in the SOC console. Similarly, this is a key security event, and should not be viewed as merely a device failure but possibly a denial-of-service attack, in that the attacker was successful in taking down a firewall, thus causing the failover event.

Repeats of this event should raise a high alert, as it would become fairly evident that something potentially malicious is occurring. This type of event would probably not have to be relayed to the NOC, as their staff probably already monitors for such an event, purely from an operations standpoint. However, the NOC "run book" should indicate that when such an event is detected, the SOC security personnel should be notified, so that both parties who would have strong interest can react in a coordinated fashion. The network group would be concerned more on the device failure and, of course, to some degree why, but the security personnel would be most concerned on why the event occurred, and was this key security component the focus of a targeted attack? The point is, as you develop components of your security alert management system, you should ensure that the right message is being delivered to the right people.

As we begin to think about the rule set for forwarding alerts to the NOC, we must keep in mind that the rules we develop for alerts must be critical enough from a security standpoint that they warrant immediate or near-immediate attention. In addition, we need to make sure that these same alerts are not already being reported under standard NOC messages. We must take into consideration the environment we will be dealing with in generating, distributing, and acting upon the alerts we plan to distribute. We want to generate only key alerts, so as not to flood the NOC and operators with a flurry of irrelevant security events that they will soon learn to ignore. Once credibility is lost, it can be very hard to regain.

So, just as we think through alerting rules for the SOC console, we must do the same for the alerts generated on the NOC console, but possibly on a more selective scale, with a higher alert threshold.

To further compare and contrast SOC versus NOC alert messages, refer to the example from our firewall logs in Chapter 3 where a message indicating denied traffic was generated. In this scenario, we would likely have a rule defined to report some high water mark for these message types to the SOC console. This rule would, of course, have to be developed over a period of time to tune the system, so as not to report each individual event (as your firewalls probably receive any number of these errors on a regular basis just due to network noise). For the NOC, we have to set a different threshold on this same rule set to determine when to send an alert of this type of event. We have to balance the risk with the business capabilities of the NOC, knowing that they are network personnel, not as focused on the security aspect of network activity and alerts.

For example, if our current rule for generating a SOC console message is set to 100 events/hour from any one firewall, then the NOC rule should be some number larger than 100, which would deem the event critical and worthy of attention. Here is where some analysis and cost benefit thoughts come into play. When does it become critical such that the enterprise is threatened and the consolidated event must be reported to get attention? Is it the 101st event that triggers an alert to the NOC or the 151st?

As previously mentioned, a balance should be struck between generating only relevant alerts to the NOC, and not missing key alerts that need near-immediate attention. One approach is to make percentage increase decisions based on experience in reviewing past log events and incidents. If we have a related or similar incident in recent history where the enterprise was indeed under attack, find what percentage increase in events occurred in that instance, and then use the results to set a benchmark for the percentage increase to decide whether to issue a high NOC alert. Granted no two attacks are alike, but at least we have used some degree of real-world data on which to base the first guess at setting a threshold. Even though it may be a guess, like all of our other settings, it involves a starting point and then some follow-up tuning to tailor the system to the environment. If we set the NOC alerting threshold to report at a 25 percent increase over your SOC alerting, then it would fire off a NOC alert for denied access when the system receives 125 denied incidents per hour. This in turn should set off a chain of events that make the system work for the enterprise based on the alert.

We've covered a lot of ground so far, including log consolidation and generating specific security events from these logs, but what needs further refinement is a process to use our existing logging correlation system, to provide potentially 7 × 24 alert reporting to the NOC (which is manned on an around-the-clock basis). Our first example, which was alerting the NOC to firewall failovers, was a fairly basic event that warranted 7 × 24 monitoring and would be of value to NOC personnel who would be responsible for monitoring general infrastructure devices on the network. The more important concept however, is how we can transfer monitoring of our security relevant events to the 24 × 7 NOC consoles, first to share the value of information we are collecting, but also to broaden the monitoring capabilities of our enterprise, including our security-specific components via this alerting mechanism.

Let's now look at other alert types that make sense to share with the NOC for some of the reasons previously stated. This second alert type would identify high rates of anomalies or detection of specific targeted attacks that would warrant immediate attention or at least acknowledgment.

Network security detection systems have grown to a degree of sophistication that they can produce relevant event detection and reporting, with a higher degree of confidence over the earlier systems, meaning fewer false positives. These systems are greatly improving and add value to the security of the infrastructure, but if we don't have trained staff to monitor and review the detections, then the system is of little use. Event collection and the correlation system should be configured to incorporate events from the IDS or IPS (intrusion prevention system) correlated against other events collected and make relevant alerts for operations personnel who may not have the in-depth security background. Using this approach, we can then write rules to generate NOC alerts when critical anomalies are detected and ensure we are getting some attention to these high alerts on an around-the-clock basis.

Let's start with some basic IDS/IPS alerts where there is a very high confidence that the alert is valid. Legacy network detection systems are signature-based, where there is a known signature of a known attack loaded into the sensors such that when a certain pattern of traffic is detected on the network, an alert is generated. The more advanced systems now not only detect and report on the traffic, but are also capable of stopping the anomalous traffic when detected, hence the intrusion "Prevention" naming convention. Although many organizations are still more than slightly hesitant to invoke this full capability, systems are becoming more sophisticated and capable of reducing the number of false positives thus giving security managers the confidence to allow these IPSs to perform their core task as programmed. With this confidence, our event collector can then have the confidence to report high-risk network traffic anomalies to the NOC.

Once again, thresholds must be set (and tuned) or events prioritized such that only high-level risk events are reported to the NOC. IDSs are known for their high degree of false positives (but that is decreasing with the current product set); nevertheless, there are still a high number of alerts generated from these systems. One feature of IPSs that can be taken advantage of is the ability to rate the risk of the anomalies detected, in a very basic state of high, medium, and low. By first monitoring our IPS directly, we can get an idea of the accuracy of the IPS alerts, and when the system is set to report only "high-risk" events, we can validate the accuracy of these alerts. We may find that some alerts shown as high risk may actually be a component of the enterprise and thus have to be filtered out from further reporting.

The point here is that by directly monitoring our IPS infrastructure, we can perform the necessary tuning to ensure it is only reporting relevant events, and then incorporate these into our security alerting up to the NOC; this is part of the initial tuning process. An example of this might be your authorized internal scanning system that is part of the security infrastructure, but because many malicious code attacks may also perform such scanning, your IPS may mistake it for one of these malicious scans and raise a high alert or red flag. You, therefore, have to reprogram your scanning tool from hitting the alerting engine to eliminate this false positive (you could mask it on the alerting tool, but this has security ramifications, which we discuss later). It is this type of tuning that should normally be performed on the IPS reporting system. This is even more important if we are going to report these incidents to our NOC consoles, again due to the fact we have to minimize the amount of false positives.

Filtering or thresholds for reporting IDS events are not necessarily based only on the number of events but also on the severity of the event captured along with a confidence level in the accuracy of the report or alert (based on your system tuning). Other examples of high-risk alerts from the IDS that should be passed over to the NOC might include high numbers of known malicious traffic traversing the network. By combining the risk factor, the confidence level (if correctly identifying this risk), and some number of events, we can then pass our alert on to the NOC with a degree of confidence that it is worthy of reporting, for example, a detection of the Slammer Worm code traversing the network. In today's world that may not be considered a high risk, but we can have high confidence of accurately detecting it as the signature is well known. Using this example, we may want to write a rule with the following thresholds set to determine whether to generate a NOC alert.

```
If event ID = SLAMMER AND Event count =>300 THEN
Write "SLAMMER Events Detected on xx.yy.xx.yy subnet"
to NOC console nn.yy via SNMP
```

Although this is not an actual rules code, this gives an idea of the alert rule that should be written to generate a NOC alert. Analysis has to be built into this rule up front because some individuals may question why we would consider an event pertaining to Slammer as relevant when all machines have been patched against it. This is a valid question for a low number of Slammer alerts or rather events being detected, however, when the number increases high enough that it can affect traffic in any set period of time, it may be an indication of a reinfection of an unpatched machine possibly recently introduced to the network. Two things now need to be addressed: finding the infected machine and removing it from the network. Even though it may not be perceived to be a great risk to the rest of the enterprise, it is still producing a potentially high amount of unwanted traffic and can possibly find another equally unpatched machine causing further impacts on the network infrastructure. The point here is that the combination of conditions are enough to warrant an NOC level alert, knowing that we have a 7 × 24 hour monitoring system established, and that this is potentially a high-risk, high-confidence alert. What we have done is supplemented our SOC abilities with NOC capabilities, leveraging off resources already available within the enterprise. We have taken care in only alerting those alerts that warrant attention and, hopefully, not overburdened our NOC personnel.

A final example of the type of events that should be considered for NOC reporting, is those having to do directly with data protection. With the explosive growth of regulatory factors over the corporation's responsibility to protect the individuals' data that they have in their possession, an equally large number of new data protection tools and approaches have emerged. Some approaches promote data detection sensors that sniff your network lines for movement of what is classified as sensitive data and raise an alert if specified volumes of that data type exit your network. These new tools fall into an emerging category of "data content analysis" engines. Other approaches to enhancing data protection within the enterprise address the perceived need to encrypt all data in transit with appliance-type boxes outside your databases holding sensitive content. Still other tools are entering the market that claim to enforce network policy by monitoring and redirecting traffic that does not match current policy (although these are still a maturing product line, but if successful should of course be closely monitored).

The point of considering the close logging and monitoring of these tools is that they all deal with your sensitive data, potentially on a real-time basis, and any failure or action of these tools could greatly affect your business processes. Or if the tools do mature and provide the intended value, then the alerts they generate would definitely warrant action. Take, for example, the emerging data content analysis tools, which are intended to monitor your network for unauthorized data leakage of your sensitive data from your network. If this category of tools matures and is able to accurately detect the unauthorized movement of your sensitive data, then the alerts from these tools would be of obvious high value. Collecting, consolidating, and correlating the logs from such tools would clearly be a benefit to the enterprise. And having the ability to search back in these logs for forensics analysis is another strong capability if these systems were included in your enterprise logging system, as you may not immediately know you have an issue when it occurs. As an example, if in an after-the-fact mode, an investigation turns up an open access in a firewall, sometime after it had occurred, then a backward-looking report query could be generated, whether any sensitive data was logged as "in transit" during the course of the open access.

The other emerging data protection tool that may warrant additional monitoring is the encryption tools, which are emerging in the form of appliances intended to front end your data repositories. An interesting design approach has emerged with these tools, in that despite the fact they are supposed to encrypt the data, it is recognized that they could adversely affect your business if they were to encounter any type of fault, and thus have options to "fail to open." This says that if a problem with their encryption capabilities emerges, then these inline appliances would continue to pass traffic, but just in the clear, the thought being that the business is more important than the need to encrypt.

Of course, these boxes would fire off their own alerts when this condition occurred, but let's look at the benefit your log consolidation system would provide. Assuming you had both systems in place, encrypted in transit boxes, and the data content analysis tools, knowing not all traffic will be encrypted, you should collect the logs and alerts from both product lines. Now in the case of a failure, not only would you get the notice of the device not encrypting, but you would also get the detection of sensitive traffic moving in the clear. This could be correlated into a single alert of medium criticality; as it is a known issue, it can be readily fixed and doesn't warrant a 1 a.m. "fire drill." Again, only by having the combination of these two systems logs can you intelligently analyze the situation and set a degree of risk (in this case low), as it is not an authorized distribution of your sensitive data, just a relaxed protection that can be fixed.

But we are getting beyond the scope of this logging project. The point here is as you introduce new security technology into your enterprise, you should consider whether it should be included in your enterprise logging and alerting effort as well.

We could go on with all the various alerts that would warrant NOC reporting, but we hope this has given you ideas of where it should be included and how it can be included from a logging and alerting concept.

In the next chapter we begin defining escalation processes based on these alerts from your logging system.

## Notes

1. Mobile devices have additional security issues with a different set of mitigating controls that must be considered in the security alerting process.
2. Vendor claims of concurrent console usage are under optimum situations, and the real world is far from these figures in reality.

## Chapter 7

# Setting Security Alert Levels and Escalation Processes

Let's now look at what to do with our multitude of events that the system can now generate. We covered collection, correlation, and intelligent interpretation of log and event data which is a large part of our picture, but we must also give thought to what to do with the events, reports, and general output once they are actually in our possession. In this section we walk through various alerting cases based on previous reporting scenarios and attempt to create a high-level response mechanism as well as an opportunity to use the data.

## Security Operations Center (SOC) Reporting

Let's begin with a basic SOC escalation process. We know that there will be varying levels of subject matter experts working in the SOC at any given point in time, and that we may need to spread this expertise out over multiple shifts. The fact that we have created predefined processes and procedures enables us to easily schedule competent staff resources that allow us to have confidence that the SOC team can handle the majority of security alert events with a standardized methodology.

Using our multiple firewall report that potentially indicates a coordinated attack on the enterprise, let's outline a hypothetical escalation process that might be developed based on our new system and its outputs. We've briefly discussed the process going from the alerting station to action or reporting, but now we go more into detail to get the maximum benefit from the system. When we approach the reporting aspect, we need to be clear on what the report(s) is(are) based; in this case the report is on firewall logs, and IDS (intrusion detection system) alarms correlated across the enterprise. Our alerts are being generated for the purpose of showing the enterprise security status and for storing the native collected logs from our specified devices.

In setting the alerts for the SOC, we must have defined alert levels that will determine various response levels. Stepping back to our reporting definition, let's use the example of a three-level alert reporting structure (typical in most commercial log correlation consoles). The lowest level alert would be a Level 3 Alert, color coded to orange; a Level 2 Alert coded to yellow; and a Level 1 Alert color coded, of course, to red.

Now the definition of each alert level needs to be defined for the environment to further guide development of the response process. Let's assume the following alert level definitions:

> *Level 1 Alert:* A real threat is identified (all the evidence programmed into the system points toward an imminent threat). There is high probability of potential damage to the system(s) or network. This threat has a highest confidence of possible damage to the system or enterprise (i.e., it probably is not a false positive).
>
> *Level 2 Alert:* A real threat is identified, but not with as high a confidence of potential damage to the system(s) or network. This is the big differentiator in that it doesn't have a high damage potential to the enterprise, but is still identified as a threat. This alert level warrants attention and possibly some form of response, as it could escalate to a Level 1 Alert.
>
> *Level 3 Alert:* This level can be considered a minor warning level, although it can be a result of two different causes. In the first instance the alert could be triggered by the detection of a very low-level threat, which by itself isn't a major threat to the system, but it is still a defined warning or possible signature of a known threat. The second cause of the alert may be due to the detection of some form of an anomaly on the system or network, which may or may not have a definition; nevertheless, its behavior makes it worthy of attention.

In both Level 2 and Level 3 Alerts, the fact that they are alerts indicates that they warrant attention. In addition because both alert categories are capable of escalating to the next alert level, some level of attention or escalation process must take place.

Assuming a Level 3 alert, we can take an example of anomalous behavior detected from a number of devices across the enterprise from which we have correlated logs. We assume that all the tuning necessary (as depicted in previous chapters) has been done, and we have high confidence that this is a real alert (based upon our strong rules engine). The alert may have been triggered by the rule that identifies similar attack signatures or even identical attack signatures coming in from a broad distribution of devices that would indicate a possible coordinated attack against the enterprise. It could also be a distributed worm or malicious code component loose within or on the perimeter of the enterprise. Because it is an anomaly, it isn't defined as a particular threat, but because it is detected on multiple systems, it warrants some degree of an alert, hence a Level 3 Alert.

Now the question comes up, what happens when SOC personnel have Level 3 alerts appear on their console? Is it time to wake up system administrators across the enterprise and call out the emergency response team? Not at this point, but it must definitely be acknowledged by SOC personnel, as they are the human component that provides the intuitive human analysis (which can't be programmed into the system—at least not yet, but there is hope that some day the "carbon-based units" will be taken out of the loop).

Most log consolidation and alert systems that incorporate a console with multilevel alerts provide some form of acknowledgment system, which allows the human components to check off or acknowledge various alerts received. For now this would be all that the operators would be doing. The fact that it was brought to the operators' attention would hopefully place it in the "thought queue" of SOC staff and recorded for potential forensic analysis (if required) sometime in the future. The system should be additionally tracking all alerts as they pass certain rules thresholds. As previously mentioned, your system tuning sets various thresholds of when to alert, and the fact it passed the first threshold and made it to a Type 3 Alert, says it must be further tracked to determine if it reaches the next level of alert which would warrant more attention. This type of acknowledgment system is a "must" requirement for our product or system selection. A manual logging mechanism for these alerts is not a feasible management method. As your system grows and incorporates many other inputs or feeds from a multitude of devices, manually or nonelectronically recording these alerts would be cost prohibitive. Another item that should be considered is an operator identifier of who acknowledged the alert. If a question comes up about the alert, reference to the original identifier can be traced back to the operator. This is also helpful in a multisite SOC, such as in a "follow-the-sun"[1] architecture where SOC responsibility rotates among different geographic sites.

There are two types of Level 3 Alerts. The initial type of Level 3 Alert may be harder to track because it doesn't have an identifying signature (it is merely an anomaly). Although one anomaly may differ from all others, it is still "strange" enough that it triggers an alert to the console. The second type of Level 3 Alert is due to the detection of a threat signature. Although not a signature of high damage probability, it is nevertheless on the radar screen as a potential threat that warrants notification. Known signatures can easily be tracked and logged and have a relatively high threshold of detection before they even become an alert.

This is where tuning comes into play. If our threshold is set so low that nearly every event or detection of this signature triggers a console message, then the messages become meaningless. Hopefully by the time we have established regular operating procedures the tuning has been set, and only those events that warrant a message and attention are getting to the console. For example, we may believe that a certain buffer overflow attack signature is relatively harmless to our environment, so we choose not to immediately alarm on that signature but we still set a reporting threshold of say, 40,000 events over a 24-hour period and then only if detected on more than three of our reporting tools (firewalls, IDS, or IPS [intrusion prevention system] devices). We're now set to record the events, but not clog our console with each event, and only report some form of an issue once the number reaches our threshold that may require some degree of attention. Furthermore, it gets recorded and acknowledged at a minimum in case it comes to the point of escalating to a Level 2 Alert due to its persistence or increase in volume, which then becomes a different type of threat to the enterprise.

With a high confidence level in our (reliable) rules engine, our SOC team can spend the effort analyzing and researching those alerts that reach their console and are worthy of at least an acknowledgment.

Let's move now to a Level 2 Alert, the next threat level up. A Level 2 Alert warrants a bit more attention and possibly human intervention or response. A Level 2 alert was defined as something that has the ability to cause harm to the system or network. This could be a progression of a Level 3 Alert or a buffer overflow attack that has already been patched, but may have been detected at 40,000 (threshold) events over a 24-hour period. Correlated from three different devices, the attack may not be an immediate threat to the network or enterprise, but if it were to escalate to a greater number of events from a number of devices, it could move to a Level 2 Alert. The basis of it being a Level 3 Alert could have been due to the fact that we did not believe that our systems were susceptible to this type of attack either due to no vulnerable devices or that patching had occurred on all known vulnerable devices. But if the attack count were to escalate, and the potential of more vulnerable devices throughout the network increase, we would now have a different type of problem, not due to the specific nature of the attack, but the sheer volume.

For example, if we set the threshold at 100,000 events from five or more devices on the same attack signature received over a 24-hour period, we may now be facing a variety of issues that warrant attention, thus escalating to a Level 2 Alert. In this scenario we are obviously under heavy attack within or possibly at the enterprise perimeter when our logging and detection systems are busy producing the logs of each of these events and our network is rapidly filling with this attack traffic. We may soon be subject to denial of service, not due to a specific vulnerability, but due to the volume of the traffic and our detection systems. Action should now be taken as this does pose a potential threat to the enterprise. There is a variety of methods by which this scenario may be addressed, but it depends on our security architecture and toolsets implemented within the enterprise. In enterprises that have not progressed or don't believe in the approach of automated intrusion prevention systems, then having this alerting and logging system is the backup to these automated tools and requires possible human intervention and response once this scenario is detected. Now we can begin to see the difference between a Level 3 and Level 2 Alert in terms of the degree of response, potential threat to the enterprise, and how a single alert can quickly escalate from one level to another.

Let's look at another example of how a Level 2 Alert gets generated. This can come where the threats are defined for the system, but there is a degree of confidence that the system is patched for them. Threats can be defined in severity by time, meaning that a threat that appeared two years ago is, we hope, much less risk than a recently defined threat. Even though we believe that we have patched for it, we may still need to elevate it to a Level 2 Alert, simply because of the potential of some "yet to be" patched machines. Figure 7.1 depicts how a single threat may move through the various alert levels based on our ability to protect against it. This example is for a single threat and how it may be alerted on in our enterprise based on our protections from this one threat.

For example, let's look at a Cisco router vulnerability in a company that is mostly Cisco-dependent for both internal and external network infrastructure components. Upon first notification that the Cisco component may be vulnerable, security system administrators should set up detection tools to secure the device(s) in preparation for the "Zero Day" threat.[2] In this scenario, any number of events detected that match to this specific threat would automatically be escalated to a Level 1 Alert. The availability and ability to apply appropriate patches or protections against the threat will determine when the alert is reduced to a Level 2 Alert (but note in our chart that it stays at a Level 1 Alert until there is confidence

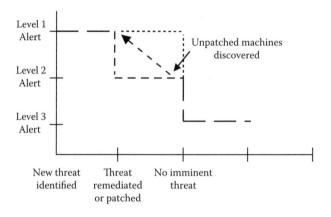

**Figure 7.1 Changing threat levels**

that the systems are patched; hence, the horizontal line at the Level 1 Alert. If no patches become available, then any detected vulnerability would stay at a Level 1 Alert in the consolidated reporting structure, all because of the imminent risk to the architecture.

Once the threat is appropriately remediated, then the alert level would be reduced to a Level 2 Alert. The alert level would then remain at Level 2 until there was a high degree of confidence that the threat was no longer a risk to the environment even though there may be a recognized "exploit" in the wild. This exploit could be malicious code that takes advantage of this identified vulnerability and therefore supports the reasoning of keeping this vulnerability at a Level 2 Alert reporting status. There could even be a re-elevation of the threat level, should you discover a re-emergence of vulnerabilities to this threat within your environment. This could be due to a newly discovered cache of unpatched machines, which is very often the case, due to faulty scans or the reintroduction of machines into your network at some later date. The open dotted line indicates this escalation of the threat back to a Level 1 Alert when this type of event occurs in the threat matrix. But it still follows the same path, once the risk is mitigated or completely patched, and is again pushed back down to a Level 2 Alert.

This last example of a Level 2 Alert shows how alerts can move down the alert level matrix versus moving up the alert level matrix as in the first example.

Last, there are threats that come right in at a Level 2 Alert. These are usually middle-of-the-road threats that may be generic in nature, or high in volume, but pose no imminent danger to the enterprise. This type of alert may not have been a Level 1 or Level 2 previously, but emerges due to a predefined alerting rule.

From these examples it should be clear how a Level 2 Alert can emerge and be identified based on the rules engine in our consolidated logging tool.

Now let's turn to how we establish response to our rules, and also what to do once the rules engine generates one of these alerts.

## The Escalation Process

With an established escalation process and appropriate tools, the SOC team comes onto the field of play and available subject matter experts emerge to perform their expert analysis as required. Many systems have canned response mechanisms based on known signatures or even behavior responses that assist the console operators. However, this information may be limited to just known signature attacks, and offer only clues (or high-level recommendations) for behavioral-based attacks because they are undefined, thus providing no firm direction on how to respond.

So now the responsibility for action falls to the console operators. The fact that we are capturing the raw logs directly from sources detecting the inputs gives the SOC team drill-down capability to the data needed to perform an analysis. Using our buffer overflow example (identified as 100,000 threshold events from four or more devices within a 24-hour period), our SOC personnel will proceed to map out exactly where these events are coming from, beginning with identifying the severity of the threat. We started out saying that one of the actions was to map out the detected threat and, in this case, it is clearly important to determine whether the event is being detected on the perimeter or on internal sources within the enterprise.

The bigger threat is obviously when it is detected on the internal network (as that obviously exposes many more devices within your enterprise and they are in the immediate path of the detected attack). Although an external detection is still important (but for a different reason), fewer devices would be exposed externally, hence, a lower risk probability. But the fact it is hitting your perimeter does make it a threat to your environment and must be addressed. Nevertheless, we would face a different problem of sheer volume of the attack (and corresponding alerts being generated). So it becomes clear that the first step of mapping out the source will warrant differing responses and degrees of urgency.

Now is where the ad hoc reporting capabilities begin to come into play in our log consolidation tool. The security analysts may not only want to know the sources of the log events that generated a Level 2 Alert, but also the volumes attributed to each alert and rate of growth as well as other details and specifics.

An escalation process may typically follow the steps outlined below to address this and other Level 2 Alerts.

1. Reported Event: Level 2 Alert reported to console.
2. Analysis: An Actionable Event that requires a security analyst's review (beyond mere acknowledgment). The analyst may be required to provide additional detail using drill-down capability to research the source, volume, and trend analysis of the event. If information is not immediately available, the analysis may require some form of ad hoc reporting, where the analyst has the ability to generate a report based on the known attributes of the event. The analyst can program a report based on the gateway IP address where most of the events were captured from, with an event ID, requesting all associated fields, or another option is to query the event type across all devices, to determine how widely the event type is occurring. This last example shows the benefits of actually having an enterprise consolidated logging system, as we don't know what we should be looking for, but having the data available from a multitude of devices makes the system capable of performing this degree of forensic security analysis.
3. Event Identification: Based on the analysis from the previous step, action must be identified and executed to appropriately react to a given alert. Possible actions include:
   a. Confirmed false positive: This type of Level 2 Alert is the easiest to identify assuming adequate SOC staff experience with the system, the environment, and general security practices. The alert may come from a recognizable source, such as an internal vulnerability scanning tool that is triggering a firewall alert which may have detected an "unauthorized" scan of its perimeter "side." Or it may be a new installation, or reconfiguration of the scanning tool, so it wasn't acting in this manner previously and thus may have shown up due to frequency or degree and breadth of detected port scanning. Another possibility is a misconfigured firewall possibly with stronger access rules that may be erroneously denying authorized/normal traffic and due to the number of denies escalated to a Level 2 Alert. These examples may be the cause of false positives, and usually can easily be acknowledged and dismissed by SOC personnel.
   b. Known threat (currently being patched for, and recently identified): The action would be to
      1) Sweep all systems subject to this vulnerability to identify any unpatched systems. Successful scans showing no more vulnerable systems would result in reducing this from a Level 2 Alert to a Level 3 Alert indicating there is no longer an imminent threat to the enterprise.

2) If only a minimal percentage of systems are currently patched for this threat, the action would be to either accelerate the rate of patching, or take risk mitigation actions (see below), and in both cases maintain or escalate to a Level 1 Alert threat condition for the identified vulnerability.

c. Unknown threat, (high in volume): The action would be to further analyze alternative approaches to block the threat either via router or firewall rules, if applicable. If these protections are available, consideration should be given to lowering the alert level to a 3.[3] (This action keeps it on the console and in the view of our SOC analysts, but not to the severity of a Level 2 Alert.)

d. Unknown threat (high in volume, minimal to <u>no available risk mitigation</u> actions identified): An Unknown Threat scenario could be described as a worst-case Level 2 Alert. If the SOC analysts confirm this as the situation, then the action would be to elevate it to a Level 1 Alert and then proceed with a Level 1 Alert escalation process (as depicted later in this chapter). This says that because there are no immediate risk mitigation actions available, it definitely warrants a high degree of attention and notifications (SOC and possibly to management).

4. Alert Acknowledgment: As a final step, we should acknowledge all alerts within the system so that there is a record of attention to the alert. This feature should be in the core requirements list early on in the evaluation of the COTS (commercial off-the-shelf) products. Most current vendors offer this capability in their default system feature list. The ability to acknowledge alerts should record not only the time and date of the acknowledgment, but also the operator who performed the acknowledgment and include an operator comments field in case there are details of the acknowledgment that should be recorded for other operators to view.

The escalation list for a Level 2 Alert provides an indication of the level of effort that is required by SOC personnel as well as how alerts can be reclassified to a different level should conditions warrant change.

Let's now delve deeper into the escalation by looking at a Level 1 Alert. In analyzing the conditions that might trigger such an alert, we can further understand how to develop an escalation process for this alert level.

# Level 1 Alerts

Level 1 Alerts were described as a threat or vulnerability that has high potential for causing damage or risk to our enterprise. From this description we know that in the event of receipt of this type of alert, we must be positioned to readily react with a targeted response. Alerts escalate to this level from a variety of different sources and rules based on previous analysis and specific defined conditions. We saw how a Level 2 Alert could be escalated to a Level 1 Alert, due to either an emerging threat or volume of threats. We also saw how the timeliness of a threat can escalate a condition(s) into a Level 1 Alert; for example, recognized or recently recognized threats almost automatically become a Level 1 Alert as depicted in Figure 7.1. As previously discussed, this would usually occur due to lack of protections immediately available to a newly discovered threat or vulnerabilities, therefore, any indication of the new threat must automatically be escalated for attention or call for action. Unlike lower-level threats and alerts, where high numbers are tolerated (possibly 50,000 to 100,000 detected events per 24-hour period), Level 1 Alerts may be triggered on much lower numbers and possibly at greater frequencies. By utilizing our near-real-time logging system, with all its various sources of data, we have the ability to narrow down the reporting and correlation to finer grains of detail necessary to detect those anomalies that would generate a Level 1 Alert.

Before we go into the escalation process for a Level 1 Alert, let's touch upon another type of Level 1 Alert that has not yet been addressed. This type of Level 1 Alert is vendor-supplied alerts that come with many COTS products. Based on historical values or signatures, many reporting systems have default alerts. These systems should be closely evaluated upon product implementation because what the manufacturer identifies as a high alert may not be relevant to our environment. This is, of course, very important with Level 1 Alerts, as we would want to minimize as many false positives at this level as possible. As part of the product analysis, we want to perform a preliminary review of this feature along with any other in-depth work and analysis of the product itself. At the point of production or near production, in consideration of our predefined Alert Levels, an in-depth review of product-generated alerts must also be conducted. Some examples of such alerts may include Level 1 Alerts based on fixed numbers of high threat volumes, previously known major vulnerabilities (such as buffer overflow attacks), high numbers of component failovers, variants of DDoS attacks, and other threats. The analysis should be into the rule sets for these certain types of attacks that may come with a COTS product selected to collect and potentially alert from across the enterprise. As much as it is important to utilize the subject matter experts developed regarding the alerting structure, based on the collection of security log events across an enterprise, it is hoped we know the traits and uniqueness of our infrastructure and can therefore make the necessary adjustments to default alerts to minimize false positives. Items that may have to be adjusted include the volumes or numbers required of an event before it becomes an alert.

For example, there is a small architectural firm with a few online offices, interconnected over the public Internet for exchange of documents/layouts with a strong need for corporate security. Although their small infrastructure may have core security components required such as firewalls, a small IDS component, encryption, and authentication components, they are most likely lacking hardened IPS components, or full-scale network compartmentalization. Thus there may be very low threshold levels set on their reporting and alerting system, as not only will traffic be low but their number of detection systems would also likely be low in number. Therefore, the firm would want to be alerted to threats or potential vulnerabilities early on when a threat is initially detected in the central logging system. They might rely heavily on vendor-supplied alerting rules as they may consider their environment fairly generic in nature. Although they may require some form of system tuning, in this scenario, starting with the vendor-supplied alerts is a feasible basic strategy. In these instances vendor-supplied default rules sets are useful, and may need only minor modifications in resetting the threshold number of events to generate an alert due to their smaller-sized environments.

However, assuming that the majority of users will be in a highly complex, distributed enterprise environment with multiple access points, compartmentalization or network segmentation, layered protections, and a variety of network security detection systems, a much higher degree of tuning of alerts has to take place, especially in the Level 1 Alert mode. As previously mentioned, vendor-supplied alerts are usually very generic and broad-based, but in more complex, larger environments, there is the need to slim down such alerts, such that only relevant alerts show up on the central console(s). This is where we have to start by identifying the type of default alerts included in the system and then determine their applicability to the environment, filtering out those that don't apply or, at a minimum, reducing their alert level so they don't transmit as a Level 1 Alert (noise in your system). This type of analysis will require work during implementation including tuning once the system is in place. The benefit in the long run is a reduction in the potential of an undo number of false positives. We show in the next section that the effort and response work required to address false positives can be a significant burden on resources and should be minimized wherever possible. Part of our analysis would start in the product selection process, possibly with a line item requirement of "Tunable Default Alerts" (indicator that a consolidated reporting system has default alerts that can be modified in the form of elimination of the alert, or alert level status changes and threshold changes, specific to the customer's environment).

Now we are prepared to look at the actual Level 1 Alert escalation process. This is a key process as this is the highest level of alert; hence we deal with issues that pose the greatest threat to the enterprise.

1. Reported Event: Level 1 Alert is reported to the console.
2. Analysis: Similar to a Level 2 Alert, it is an actionable event, thus requiring a security analyst's review (beyond a mere acknowledgment). The analyst will be required to conduct some form of analysis with some form of drill-down capability to research the source, volume, and trend analysis of the event. If this is not immediately available via drill-down capabilities, it may require some form of ad hoc reporting where the analyst has the ability to generate a report based on the known attributes of the event. The analyst will need to program a report based on the gateway IP address where the most events were captured from, with an event ID, and request all associated fields, or the analyst may query the event type across all devices to determine how widely the event type is occurring. In some cases as we show below, a report keyed to all fields may have to be generated as there may not be an identifiable known attribute or fingerprint for the event. This last example shows the benefits of actually having an enterprise consolidated logging system, as we don't always know what we should be looking for, especially for new anomaly events that are escalated to Level 1 Alerts. This is where a comprehensive logging system provides the most benefit, as SOC staff has at their fingertips the maximum available data from which to conduct their forensic analysis. This may not be the case if we have filtered out too much data. Earlier we spoke of the configuration and filtering process in an effort to make the overall system more efficient or to minimize the overall impact on the network. This is where tuning comes into play and is clearly an ongoing process. During the course of an investigation of a Level 1 Alert, we may find that there is not enough data and may require more input to identify the cause of the event. A feedback for system enhancements should be part of the process that we speak to later in this chapter.
3. Event Identification: Based on the analysis coming from the previous step, hopefully the event type that triggered the alert in the system could be identified. Next, an action must be identified and executed upon to appropriately react to the alert. Possible event types that may be identified are as follows.
    a. Confirmed false positive: Hopefully, our system was tuned enough to filter out most false positives from reaching a Level 1 Alert, however, this event may be more difficult to identify

at this point, because any event that reaches a Level 1 Alert has already passed various level checks for volume, vulnerability, or threat and frequency thresholds. Similar to false positives at Level 2, there may be clear reasons why the event escalated to Level 1 and, therefore, the confidence to dismiss these alerts by knowledgeable SOC staff without a great amount of in-depth analysis, especially if the source address is from an internal tool. Just as the cause may be a misconfiguration either on our detection system(s), or one of our protection tools (firewalls), it can be cause for corrective actions and reconfiguration requests to keep the alert from popping up again. An alternative remediation action may be to mask out alerts that are generated by these devices (where "masking out" means that we program our detection devices to ignore any alerts coming from this source). Although this may cause another problem as we know, for example, that network vulnerability scanning tools will repeat the process on a regular basis and thus continue to set off sensor alerts. If masking isn't done on the detector and the scanner isn't configured to continually skip scanning that sensor, then masking could be done on the reporting system. The security risk with this concept is that now we have a blind spot in our detection architecture illustrated in the following scenario. Scanning a network by a malicious person, code, or worm is a by-the-book hack, as they usually start with the discovery phase of the attack. Scanning is the easiest automated method to execute a discovery phase. As attacks have gained sophistication, they now try to mimic known scanning tools on the network in the hopes that just such a blind spot was established in the detection and reporting tools such that any scanning performed by these devices now goes unnoticed. The potential attacker would attempt to find these authorized scanning systems, and then take over their identity and perform their own data gathering scans under the radar and watchful eye of the enterprise's reporting systems. So when staff identifies a false positive Level 1 Alert that is based on authorized tools within the system, caution should be taken in merely blocking out further alerts and instead looking at various threshold setting techniques that don't totally mask out that system but rather set high water marks, or possibly common windows of availability for the tool to perform its scans (if such a schedule can be established). Then, if scans are detected outside those parameters, an alert will still be generated indicating the presence of the type of sophisticated attack just described. Last, once the Level 1 Alerts have been positively confirmed as false positives, they can now be dismissed and recorded as acknowledged and remediated.

b.  Known Threat: If of the type currently being patched for and recently identified but because it is still classified as an imminent threat, it must therefore be elevated to a Level 1 Alert. This type of reclassification from a Level 2 Alert was discussed in the previous sections because it now has a much greater risk level to the enterprise and is deemed worthy of more attention and reaction by the analysis team. Reasons may be due to the fact that many systems were found to be still vulnerable to a particular threat either due to the lack of patching or incomplete patch processes. In this scenario, the escalation should be cause for acceleration of the patch process, if possible, with evidence of the threat to the environment supported by the number of alerts that the SOC is receiving on the console. In addition, there should be management notification of the severity of the threat (although we speak later on utilizing the system for management level reporting), but at this point it should just be noted as an action in response to the Level 1 Alert and included as part of the escalation process. Other remediation or escalation processes may include increased vigilance over the consoles and/or increased frequency of alert reporting. If reporting is normally generated in batch mode, it may have to be executed more frequently or potentially converted to real-time for a temporary period of time. This increase in vigilance may be on targeted systems such as vulnerability scanning tools if it is correlated into the system to indicate unpatched systems. Similarly, reporting tools could be programmed to filter for a specific threat and only report the number of unpatched systems focused on a specific vulnerability. These targeted reports could then be run on an hourly basis to provide not only SOC staff but also the patch management team with an enterprise progress report giving an indication of how quickly the vulnerability is being remediated through the patch process. Again the benefits of incorporating a broad variety of enterprise security tools into a centralized logging method can be of great benefit to the SOC during times of high threats. The key point here is awareness of going through these scenarios at an early stage and knowing where we want to be in the future. Having this information can significantly help in product selection from a scalability and capabilities perspective.

c. Unknown threat (either by a resemblance to signature of a known threat, or wholly unknown detection or anomaly): With some of the new detection systems anomalies are detected through behavior-based systems that don't rely on known signatures but rather are based on detected network or system behaviors that indicate the presence or actions of malicious code. As we show in the analysis section, these types of detected events are more difficult to protect against as we find that beyond detection of the event, there is little additional detail of what to look for when researching the cause of an event and any potential remediation actions. This is an example of worst-case scenarios and is usually a result of Level 2 Alert escalation. However, it may not only be a result of a next level upward escalation; it can also immediately emerge as a Level 1 Alert simply due to the volume, frequency, or even potential damage based on the alerts generated from virus detection systems, IDSs, or IPSs (if any or all of these console reporting mechanisms are incorporated into your consolidated logging and reporting tool). The process of how to analyze this type of event (especially if it cannot be confirmed as a false positive early on in the process) must now be dealt with as an imminent threat to the enterprise. SOC staff will need all available tools from the consolidated logging product to perform their analysis. They will need in-depth drill-down capability from the console, as well as the ability to perform a wide variety of ad hoc reporting against any and all attributes of the alert and systems logs that had any part in generating the alert. It is important when dealing with this type of Level 1 Alert that during the course of the analysis process, a record is kept of all reports and output for possible deferred forensics or potential prosecution if it is found to be a genuine focused attack against the enterprise by an identifiable person or entity. All generated reports whether automatic or ad hoc must have the ability to be saved and archived for later analysis or evidence. Although the evidence aspect may be difficult to prove, at a minimum it can be used internally for after-the-fact investigative purposes if it is found to be a genuine attack. This turns up yet another requirement that should be included during product selection, "System must support offline storage/archive of generated reports." Continuing down the escalation task list, just as in a Level 2 Alert, although more important in the case of a Level 1 Alert, notification or escalation to various management teams must be initiated due to perceived severity of the event(s) and threat level. There should be a predefined distribution list, method of distribution, and procedure for data classification and protections assigned to the alert data, especially if it is to be distributed outside the SOC console system. A report of "Unknown, confirmed high volumes of malicious behavioral attacks identified on all perimeter firewalls" might not be something we would want freely passed around the network. Many log and event consolidation systems have the ability to automatically generate e-mail notification, but these, at best, should only be used to alert direct SOC and NOC staff, and general security team members. It is not recommended for management notifications due to the automatic nature (caution should always be used in external notification, such as PDAs and Smartphones which is discussed further on in this chapter). It is recommended that all management notifications be generated by carbon-based units (people), as the last thing we would want is to have an automatic notification generating a slew of false positive e-mail messages (this may not be a career-enhancing move). Finally, acknowledgment of a Level 1 Alert may only be a comment on the alert, as it cannot be closed or dismissed until the full resolution is found or implemented.

Thus far we have identified some of the tasks associated with an escalation process to address alerts generated as a result of log collection inputs from a multitude of security tool sets. It is very important to have these processes predefined before deploying the system, as it would be an incomplete deployment to merely generate data without direction or guidance on how to make use of it in the real world. Figures 7.2 and 7.3 recap the escalation processes that could be used to establish an internal event or console alert message.

Recognizing that these processes are fluid and ever-changing, as the SOC team learns more about how to handle events once they experience them in the context of their specific environment, these are merely starting points for the initial deployment of a usable system. As we begin to speak to management reporting in the next section, this process is a very generic term in an escalation process, but once we begin operating the processes, we can add details to the task. Management reporting may not only include senior IT management, but possibly legal counsel if it is found to be an actual attack and, through team analysis, that the attacker is identified and vulnerable to prosecution.

Also be aware that other effects of an escalation process may result in the need to modify IT management processes. We may also find that

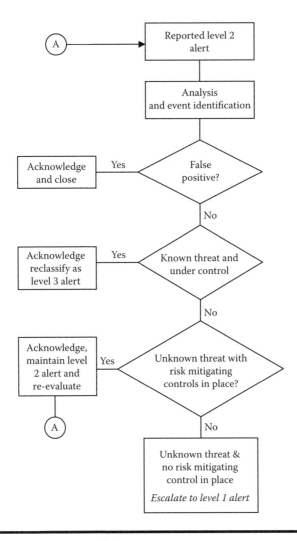

**Figure 7.2  Level 2 Alerts escalation process**

even with extensive tuning of the alert process, false positive alerts continue to pop up on the console. This could be due to the introduction of new processes and procedures, new devices on the network, or even the elimination of certain devices from the network. In all cases our logging and alerting system detected some form of change that matched the alerting rule set and resulted in a console alert message. Upon further analysis, the team found that it was indeed a false positive due to actions by an authorized party somewhere else in the enterprise. Based on these findings, we may have to implement a broader communication mechanism alert to all SOC or NOC staff concerning changes beyond their immediate

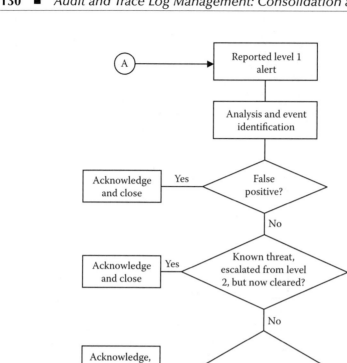

**Figure 7.3 Level 1 Alerts escalation process**

environment because we now have a window on the enterprise, and hence alerts on the enterprise. In established network enterprises this may simply involve getting SOC staff added to the change management system as an approver or possibly as a "notified party" of enterprise-level changes, just so the team is aware and in the event of an alert detection of some form of change either through increased traffic loads or new protocols, the information can be correlated with a recently introduced (authorized) change.

The ideal scenario is to have the change management system's inputs automatically correlated into the log consolidation system; however, the complexity of preparing correlation rules between two disparate systems may be beyond the current capabilities of products available in the marketplace today. This is one of those "futures" that we talk about in Chapter 8.

## Management Reporting

The management reporting aspect of a logging system may seem trivial, but experience shows that it can be one of the most critical points beyond first-level alerting and reporting. By showing that SOC and even NOC staff have the ability to make use of all security tools (or the vast majority of them) in a single reporting system can be an overwhelming show of competence to a management team. In this section we touch on some of the different methods that can be used to perform management reporting while leveraging the system to its fullest potential. In the previous section we alluded to some instances where management reporting was a critical component of the escalation process; as such, it should be part of the standardized escalation process.

When looking at management reporting, the description pretty much says it all: the target audience is management. It is a report that has to convey the message in a very small sound bite (or view), there must be a high confidence level of reliability, and there must be the ability to provide further depth of the information should it be requested (management may have risen through the ranks and have the technical capability to request further detail and analysis information). The report should have the ability to be generated on the fly as some management reporting is triggered by certain alert levels. When reached in critical mass, senior management must be notified in order to cover the assets of the reporting or analysis team should the event escalate to a real enterprise threat to the point of interrupting business processes. In such cases it is common to hear the management question, "How long have we known about this?" By having a management notification system and process built into the escalation procedures, it becomes common practice when events escalate to a level of a high threat potential.

Following are some examples of this level of reporting where it is necessary to convey to the management team that there are escalating threats to the enterprise, and that the SOC/NOC team is aware of it, and the threat was critical enough to notify management of the situation.

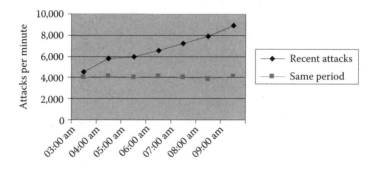

**Figure 7.4 Trend analysis of an attack**

In our first example we looked at an attack and showed it was identified on a growth trend specific to our environment. We also contrasted it with the normal trend of this type of attack in the "Same Period" line item, and showed that "Recent Attacks" clearly indicated a high growth rate while highlighting the apparent trend over the time period (shown in hours in Figure 7.4).

A couple of key items need to be pointed out on how to present this type of report to management. We obviously don't want to generate escalation reports on a daily basis as they would quickly lose their impact. We would, however, reserve the report for the actual time that we need management attention or have a high concern that the issue could become a real problem for the enterprise. The attack should be shown in the context of time and degree of risk. In our example we did this by showing the consolidated report hypothetically across "All West Coast Data Centers." The report indicates that the incident times are shown in Pacific Standard Time (PST). This is key as it shows a broad attack covering multiple data centers and shown in local time to those locations, which is relevant as it appears to be on the increase at the beginning of the West Coast business day, making this a key concern. In the report, we have only provided data deemed relevant to the incident for management review, and have intentionally not given too much data that could potentially cloud the issue. We did not drill down to the event type (i.e., actual error code or event type, specific numbers, but only graphical representations) or event sources (or types of sources), nor did we include any protocols, ports, or other identifying specifics of the event. This type of data isn't relevant for high-level management reports. Our goal is simply to convey to management that the SOC/NOC has identified an attack that is growing in size, and its target seems to be a significant portion of the enterprise and is currently in progress at the beginning of the business day.

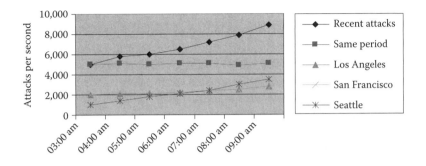

**Figure 7.5  Trend analysis of a distributed attack**

We can always provide more level of detail, but again, keep in mind it is a management report so the detail should be directly relevant to the audience. The additional detail provided in Figure 7.5 is a management report on the same incident but broken down by the specific (hypothetical) West Coast data centers; this report would be going to the management at each of those local offices and is obviously more relevant because it relates to their specific numbers.

Because we are consolidating the firewall reports from multiple points (such as these three data centers), we know where the records are from and can create an aggregate report of the detected attack. For management we can just reverse the aggregation process. In preparing the report, the same presentation topics apply, showing that the "Same Period" versus the "Recent Attacks" line is on the rise, but now is also showing activity by individual data centers where we can point out that all data centers are experiencing increased attack counts for a particular incident. In this example, the emphasis should be given to the Seattle data center as it is seeing the highest growth rate and could soon be experiencing a denial-of-service issue due to the sheer volume of attacks. This may be cause for further report requests by management, as they may not have been aware of the situation and may not have taken a vested interest in the mitigation procedures or analysis of the event, hence a request for a more detailed report specific to their site.

Both of these examples show the need to have a fully functional log consolidation system that not only collects and alerts but also has a high degree of reporting capability, both standardized and ad hoc for custom-generated reports when the conditions warrant it. These are samples of very high-level escalation reports that should be part of the standardized processes that are established for our analysis teams utilizing our consolidated logging tool.

The other benefit of reporting that will come from this tool is better general status reports of the enterprise from a security monitoring aspect. Because we now have a better view of our distributed security tools, we can more easily roll up and consolidate the status of these tools into single report views. Most enterprises have standardized status report cycles for all aspects of their IT enterprises, and usually the security groups are no different. Depending on the criticality of the report, security status reports can range from daily to monthly reports depicting the nature of security events monitored, attack counts, virus eradications, service denials, and other critical enterprise security status elements. Also, because our team is actively responding to these events in an enterprise fashion, we can report team metrics such as "Number of Events Acknowledged," with an explanation of what an acknowledgment entails. Remember that we required the systems to not only collect and alert to specific event types, but also provide for the ability of SOC staff to acknowledge events on the console showing that a carbon-based unit recognized the event, and has possibly taken necessary remediation action. By reporting on the number of acknowledgments, we can show the team productivity specific to events on the monitored network. This information is, of course, important to the local management team as well as to external sources who must also validate that the network infrastructure is appropriately monitored from a compliance and security perspective.

The compliance aspect is a new reporting area to some industries. In legacy banking financial services and security exchanges, regulatory compliance is a part of doing business. With the explosion of regulatory compliance legislation in recent years, nearly all industries are now affected by new compliance mandates. In nearly all of the new regulatory mandates there is some aspect of system integrity or control and required evidence of same. This is also an area where management and system reporting from a log consolidation tool can also be very practical and beneficial. To show compliance with many of the regulatory mandates, there is usually some form of an audit, either external or a self-audit where compliance must be shown with the mandate. This "proof" can come in the form of evidence of either documented system controls, or monitoring systems to ensure the controls are working and systems are not at risk.

Just by the fact that we can show the collection of logs from a majority of distributed security systems is an indicator of a high degree of monitoring across the enterprise. By further showing report outputs that cover all these systems (such as found in Figure 7.4, which covered all West Coast data centers, and clearly shows a degree of vigilance across a broad swath of devices and locations), we can use system output as documented evidence of enterprise-level monitoring of network control devices. We later talk about how this can help our overall project, but for the purpose of management reporting, it should be recognized that it not only fulfills basic internal reporting requirements, but can also be utilized for rapidly emerging external regulatory compliance reporting requirements.

As just depicted, our logging, alerting, and reporting system if successfully implemented in a broad-based manner will find many uses across the enterprise. Compliance reporting is just one aspect; other areas will quickly emerge and our team should be prepared to capitalize on the opportunity to provide a useful and relied-upon tool for other enterprise users.

We may find it easy to generate reports that have value to another group because the data was collected in a central location and we have the ability to generate custom or targeted reports. Even though we initially captured the logs from a security-related system with the goal to correlate it with other security devices, there may also be certain user bases that would like to aggregate the data within their environment, but previously didn't have the capacity or reporting capability.

One likely candidate might be the desktop support team who would have an obvious interest in the health and welfare of the desktops in the enterprise; at best they may have a machine asset inventory report, and maybe access to the virus DAT updates performed and possibly also the eradications. But because we are also capturing internal attacks, if the attack is detected from a desktop source, this information could be useful to the desktop support team who can in turn be proactive in their response knowing that a particular machine is behind in its updates or out of compliance from its standard software suite or other such desktop configuration. Up to now, desktop support had no idea that such data was available and thus wouldn't ask for it; but due to the fact that it is now in one place and can generate a report of just desktop support relevancy, we can now gain another customer of your tool, without much added cost in generating the report, although some caution must be taken in signing up for too much reporting when you look at these additional user groups. In this example of providing desktop-related alerts to the desktop support team, it would be best to generate these reports in a batch mode (scheduled), and automated such that they don't add undue burden on your SOC staff. Additionally you may need to assign a SOC representative to the desktop staff. Should questions come up, they have a direct contact for further information, and they are not just calling anyone and everyone within your SOC.

It soon becomes obvious that our infrastructure will not only fill needs, but also add value to groups previously dealing with limited information. As we proceed in our deployment we quickly discover different parties of groups across the enterprise that can benefit from the system and its reporting capabilities. The downside to this is that it will add some overhead to the team dealing with an additional customer base. However, if the tool is developed with a strong enough user interface and easily generated reports that can be scheduled once initially programmed, then the benefit could potentially outweigh the costs of managing the system. Another potential issue is if the new customers want more than mere scheduled reports, and start asking for ad hoc reporting or special queries. Only if the organization has some form of internal cost recovery mechanism such as cross-functional charging for time and labor, can we at least artificially recover the cost of providing these services to different departments within the organization.

A final area of reporting either in escalation reporting or management reporting lies in the arena of "out of system" type reporting. This can be described as reports or alerts that are distributed outside the standard processing channels, such as to PDAs or Smartphones, that would obviously entail some form of wireless communication and most likely a third-party carrier system. Although these devices may be corporate assets, the transport of the data/message and control of the device is well outside the bounds of normally protected systems. Special care must be taken when including these devices in a consolidated logging and alerting system as an output mechanism. As previously mentioned, sending a Level 1 Alert to one of these types of devices is risky at best and should be treated with much caution.

Unfortunately the use of such mobile devices is a fast-growing aspect of the corporate infrastructure. The use of these devices for messaging, contact lists, memos, and overall corporate communication has become a pervasive tool in the corporate culture. But as we begin enhancing the alerting process and confirm the ability to develop important security alerts that the user community may want delivered via a mobile broadcast infrastructure, we become faced with even more issues in a secure (or insecure) environment.

We spoke earlier about the potential need to encrypt the transport of data, and now we are speaking of the alerts generated from the correlation of this data and considering broadcasting this same information out over free space transmission to some device possibly lacking the appropriate access controls (i.e., user identification/authentication) necessary to ensure that these sensitive messages are being delivered to the appropriate person. And beyond the risk of mere transmission of such messages, there is the storage aspect on the mobile device itself. Many now come with extensive memory capabilities, and thus the messages sent to these devices may stay on the device for quite some time. A simple review of messages received on one of these devices could provide a chronological account of system alert messages by the date and time stamp of when they were received. We cannot deny the value of having near-real-time alerts and the ability to potentially get these messages to the right person any-time/anywhere, but a balance must be struck between the risk of doing so and the benefit to the enterprise. We must anticipate such requests once consolidated logging and alerting systems are deployed, and be prepared to either stand by a "Not Possible" response, or have some risk mitigation plans to enable providing this service, but in a minimized risk method.

Some of the risk mitigation controls that could be applied include a separate mailing list for those devices that are known to be in the wild because they are wireless or of a small form factor and thus not subject to the standard corporate access and physical security controls. This specialized mailing or alerting list would only get minimal information in a one-way feed (i.e., no drill-down, obviously) with alerts or messages from the central console. Without getting too complex, we could develop some form of encoding (English readable) that would mask the true meaning of the message to the casual viewer, but still indicate the nature of the alert. (No, you won't be giving out the message, "The cats are at the west door," trying to indicate a high level of attacks on the West Coast!) Rather we could use some form of identifiers unique to the organization, such as a PBX prefix specific to that location, or other company specific office identifier. Or you could use some form of generally available identifier to form a message that might read "Level 1 message for site 408" to relate a high-level alert for the West Coast data center in area code 408. Take note that it doesn't immediately sound any alarms as the word "alert" was removed from the message and the 408 is not specified as an area code so to the unfamiliar reader this message appears innocuous. Taking these types of actions attempt to mitigate some of the risk of a console message going outside the confines of the company traversing an external uncontrolled network, and being placed on a portable device outside the confines of the physical site security.

By now we can clearly see the value of the system, and how its scope can increase even during the development phase, but more so during the deployment phase (especially when it can show its value to a variety of users across your enterprise). This latest example is not necessarily a new user base but rather a new delivery medium, which is probably going to be an obvious requirement in any large enterprise today, due to the proliferation of wireless devices. In our next section we explore more benefits of our system, but more from a "project selling" perspective, knowing that to kick off a new project on an enterprisewide basis, we need broad organizational support or buy-in. Broad buy-in and support will also help in deciding whether to even go forth with the project as assessed in terms of the current situation and make some rough cost-benefit analysis and decisions.

## Notes

1. Under a "follow-the-sun" design, the alerting or monitoring is handed off to different geographically located data centers, so the monitoring team is working during the normal workday. A U.S. West Coast data center may hand over the management at the end of their day to the Asia Pac region, which would be the beginning of their day, and then they would hand it over to the European office at the end of their day.

2. Instances where an identified vulnerability can become an immediate threat due to nearly instantaneously released attack scripts.

3. The more paranoid security analyst may choose to keep it at a Level 2 Alert just to keep an eye on it, especially if no direct patch was applied; a question we should ask is, "What degree of security paranoia characterizes our organization?"

# Chapter 8

# Pulling It All Together and Making Your Case

You should now have a fairly good idea of the type of system that you would like to build (or how to enhance components of your existing system) for the purpose of producing an enterprise-capable consolidated logging and alerting tool. Now the problem presents itself: how are you going to get the necessary funding and project team together to actually execute this grand plan. In the long run this should clearly be a benefit to your enterprise, including not only the security groups, and, as we have shown, other IT groups within your organization, but how can you justify it to your core team and the overall program groups? Early in Chapter 1 we touched on just why you would want to go down this path, but here we go into more depth.

In this section we illustrate various strategies for creating buy-in for your overall system and approach, as well as highlighting various cost-benefit analysis scenarios. We need to be able to communicate the many corporate drivers for putting such a system in place and point out the potential impact of not making such a system an inherent part of your corporate IT infrastructure.

Let's start with the very basic system analysis of consolidating four distributed enterprise firewalls to develop a costing model for the security logging and management of this distributed architecture. In a basic scenario, the following firewall logging tasks would come into play for each firewall (these are high-level tasks):

- Ensure the capture and maintenance of the firewall logs at an accessible point.
- Ensure that some daily review tool or technology is available to conduct some form of review of the logs on a daily basis.
- Ensure the logs are archived in some manner for the required retention period (30, 60, 90 days or more) consistent with your current policy statements.
- Ensure the availability of some form of a forensic analysis tool that can be used to analyze the archived logs should the need arise during the allotted retention period.
- Ensure that documentation of the process is in place and that it functions in order to prove that the processes exist and are executed (e.g., in order to meet audit requirements).

These are the most basic tasks required to meet minimal auditing requirements for this theoretical example. These would have to occur on each of the firewalls; without some form of consolidated logging or collection system in place, the costs of these tasks would be quadrupled in a four-host or firewall environment. Now compare what the tasks would be under a more consolidated environment. They would basically still be the same tasks, but only executed once. Although it's not exactly one-fourth the cost, as there would be the set-up and system acquisition, the ongoing savings would offset the cost distribution and benefit over time. Table 8.1 illustrates a high-level cost comparison of the ongoing work on a per-month basis. What isn't factored into the sheet are the set-up time and system acquisition costs, but they can be amortized, and actually the cost per system would decrease as new systems were added, and thus these costs would be further amortized.

Even these basic figures illustrate the cost advantage of consolidating the log collection and monitoring effort. A few words on this simple cost model: this assumes that most of the work is done manually by the local firewall administrator. On a daily basis the administrator should have some form of a review process over the daily logs checking for abnormalities, identified attacks, high volumes of denies, and possible failover events in the instance of mirrored firewalls. The issue of mirrored firewalls also raises a point in the number of devices, because if you are doing four gateways, initially there may be only four firewalls, but in some redundant environments this may actually result in eight firewalls, due to a failover firewall being put into place.

For the purposes of this analysis example we do not assume there is any mirroring taking place and thus cost it against just four firewalls, but in the real world you may often find this type of redundancy and will have to account for the added volume and data feeds in your architecture.

**Table 8.1    Distributed Log Monitoring Costs versus Consolidated Log Monitoring Costs**

| Monthly Cost Calculation | Daily | Monthly |
|---|---|---|
| **Under a Distributed System** | | |
| Capture and collect (locally) | Automated* | Automated* |
| Daily review (0.5 hr @ 150/hr) | $75.00 | $1,500.00 |
| Monthly archive (1 hr @ 150/hr) | | $150.00 |
| One monthly investigation (1.5 hrs @ 150/hr) | | $225.00 |
| One firewall monthly labor | | $1,875.00 |
| Four firewalls monthly labor for logging on each individually (distributed) | | $7,500.00 |
| **Under a Consolidated System** | | |
| Capture and collect (locally) | Automated* | Automated* |
| Daily review (1.5 hr @ 150/hr) | $225.00 | $4,500.00 |
| Monthly archive (programmed) | Automated* | Automated* |
| One monthly investigation (2 hrs @ 150/hr) | | $150.00 |
| Four consolidated firewalls monthly labor estimate | | $4,650.00 |
| **Annual Cost Calculation** | | |
| Distributed logging monthly cost | $7,500.00 | |
| Consolidated logging system cost | $4,665.00 | |
| **Monthly** savings | $2,835.00 | |
| Distributed logging annual cost | $90,000.00 | |
| Consolidated system annual cost | $55,980.00 | |
| **Annual** Savings | $34,020.00 | |

*Automated = automated process, no ongoing labor cost associated

Because this is a manually managed logging system, it is assumed that the monthly archival of the logs to an offline storage medium is also a manual process and this time is accounted for in these labor totals.

And finally there is the assumption that the local firewall administrator may be called upon to conduct or support an investigation, which will cause him to perform a review over his past month's logs. The incident may not be directly against his firewall; it may be an enterprisewide event, but it will still be cause for each of the local firewall administrators to review his logs to confirm involvement or no involvement, and thus each has to assume this labor cost and account for it on a monthly basis.

Under the consolidated model, these same functions take place, but there has been some form of automation, and with consolidation, the ability to perform these tasks once, covering all four systems. The capture and collection would be automated as part of the implementation of a consolidated logging system, as we related earlier in the design phase. The daily review would still occur in the form of the logging and alerting console and the time specified for this particular group of systems would be more than the single system, but still not the total hours of all four done individually. The monthly archive would also be automatic, as it would be an inherent part of the consolidated logging system, and can be achieved much more easily with all the data in one central location.

The final monthly labor task item would be the time devoted to possible investigations. Note that there is only one investigation assumed, and in our individual firewall tasking, we did the investigation four times, once for each firewall. The difference is that we can do that single investigation only once when all the system logs are combined, but under the distributed systems, each firewall administrator must look at his or her local logs individually to "investigate" whether the local system was involved. We did account for more time to conduct the investigation just due to the potential volume of data, but recall we will have a search tool available under the consolidated system and thus still be able to sort through the aggregated data in a manageable and timely fashion. (In actuality, the investigation time in your consolidated system could be much lower because it has the ad hoc search capability over the totally correlated records, but for the purpose of this example we still estimate high.)

So building on this model of the ongoing monthly cost comparison between a distributed logging system among four firewalls, versus the consolidation of those four, shows a clear cost benefit for the consolidated approach. Table 8.1 sums up this comparison between these two approaches. Extrapolating to the 12-month budget cycle, it becomes clearly evident there is a cost advantage, showing the 1-month cost savings and then the accumulated 12-month cost savings.

This is merely an illustration from the postimplementation cost perspective; what really has to be shown is the added capability the system brings to the enterprise and better security your team can offer to the enterprise when such a system is put into place. This is the "benefits" side of your project and there are obvious benefits that have been clearly identified up to this point and should be noted here when you prepare to make the proposal to put such a system in your enterprise.

We talked about the consolidation benefit, the added value of the data once it is correlated from a security perspective, but there are other tangible benefits that we only touched on earlier and these are in the area of regulatory compliance. As the regulatory environment in the corporate world becomes ever more complex, enterprises today must do their best to maintain compliance, as noncompliance is now becoming more costly and likely to be identified due to an increase in audits. Previously, you may have been audited occasionally against your own audit and control rules or policies, but now this has taken a giant leap forward as more and more external entities, be it government, industry, or localized entities, exert regulations concerning your organization. Part of the compliance issue is being able to adequately show that you have controls in place, and that they are working.

Even financial regulations are getting into the act, as the Sarbanes–Oxley (SOX) Act now places requirements on IT management as part of this compliance act. This act is targeted at ensuring appropriate financial controls are in place over publicly traded organizations, but Section 404 of this initiative calls for the ability for auditors to attest to the "accuracy of internal financial controls." Given that in today's world most financial information is based on IT systems, the accuracy of that data is reliant on strong IT controls and protections to ensure the accuracy of the data they are holding. Section 404 of the SOX Act has become one of the new drivers to IT security for the purpose of maintaining compliance. Unfortunately because the SOX Act is a financial act, it does not give any clear direction regarding what is required as a result of Section 404, but merely indicates the need to maintain "an adequate control infrastructure." This has been interpreted to mean that the IT group is responsible for maintaining their systems in a manner that an auditor can attest to these controls being in place. Your project's link to all this is the fact that you now have and maintain audit records of the systems' activity, access, and overall "health" on the network through your consolidated collection of these audit records. You have logs collected that show that access is being denied to unauthorized parties and you have logs that show the activity of the system via access records for domain authentications, and even the "who" of the access, which is important to show that only specified parties are allowed access to your network or infrastructure. All these managed security audit records can be utilized during the course of a SOX audit to show the workings of your internal "control infrastructure," supporting Section 404, and indicating the effectiveness of your internal control infrastructure.

Many COTS (commercial off-the-shelf) log consolidation systems on the market today have latched onto this connection and now sell themselves as SOX compliance tools. Granted this is true to a degree, but it is only a part of what they can do, and shouldn't be relied upon as the sole tool for SOX compliance, but they do contribute to meeting the SOX compliance issue, specifically for Section 404. Some COTS logging products even have SOX templates, which attempt to summarize the controls in place, so as you look to the commercial off-the-shelf arena for your log consolidation tool, this would be yet another requirement line item, to determine whether they provide boilerplate templates specific to SOX compliance. Additionally, because they may be generic in nature, there should be the ability to customize these templates to your specific environment, while still maintaining some degree of SOX compliance flavor.

This whole compliance issue should not be overlooked when you are building your business case for initiating a project for architecting an infrastructure audit log consolidation system. In addition to the SOX regulations, as you are probably aware, there is a multitude of regulatory issues facing the large enterprise business today. Nearly all of these regulatory mandates require some form of IT reporting or identify that the IT reporting can be a contributing factor to achieving compliance or at least supplying evidence of compliance in some form or fashion. The regulations are too numerous to go through; the point here is that you can use the compliance slant to aid in gaining the support for your infrastructure as it will clearly play a role.

## Justifying Your System for Forensic Analysis

An additional area that can be used as a justification for your system comes from the forensics side of the house. A rapidly growing area in the regulatory field comes in the form of consumer protection acts. Over the past few years, there has been an increase in documented losses of personal, or consumer personal, information by large entities. In response to this, there has been legislation enacted that mandates that companies provide better protection over Nonpublic Personal Information (NPI), and if necessary the need to disclose to their users when there is a belief that NPI data may have been compromised. This is where your log consolidation system may come into play as a forensics tool, if not identifying the breach up front, but during the course of the investigation to determine if such a disclosure is necessary. In the latter case your system can be used after any suspected breach either in response to some regulation or merely for the investigation of a suspected attack. The term "forensic" has become associated with the art and science of legal evidence and argument, thus the investigation of a suspected breach should include any and all evidence if such a breach of your systems or enterprise occurred.

Where better to start in your search than your consolidated logging system, which may prove whether such evidence exists.

We can cover a lot of ground here, linking the compliance issue, NPI, and forensics, but once you step back you can see that the three are all deeply related and your audit log consolidation system is the keystone for addressing all three. The compliance side defines the requirements at a high level; one of the target areas is the protection of NPI data of which many corporations find themselves being the "guardian." The ability to conduct computer forensics over this data becomes a firm requirement should any suspected compromise occur.

Without going into much detail we can give a few short examples of how forensics can be applied to your system, which again translates into supporting justification of building or enhancing your system.

Computer forensics can be understood as the investigation of a computer-based crime utilizing the tools and techniques to build evidence and proof that a crime did or did not occur. In our case we are going to apply it to the suspected breach of your system or enterprise and one of the main tools that we utilize is your consolidated audit log system. Such an investigation could be initiated internally or, in the worst-case scenario, externally, meaning that some outside entity has notified you that your systems have been breached and they have some evidence or data to prove it.

Whichever case it is, it is time to start gathering evidence from the systems you have, to validate whether such a breach has occurred and attempt to find the source. You would, of course, start with the suspect system potentially involved and then broaden the scope of your data collection in ever-growing concentric circles around that suspect system.

In a best-case scenario, you may have the target host name that you suspect may have been compromised, and thus have a good starting point for your data queries. Of course with this host name, you would then resolve it to the IP address, which can then easily be queried against in your logging database. You would have this IP as a source (and potentially a destination address) in your consolidated logging database. It could be the source of outbound requests going through your firewall; it could be the destination of allowed or denied requests through your firewall as well. And depending on the nature of the host, it may have log records of user access from or to the host for authentication or other system access. And as we have spoken of before, if you are also collecting your antivirus enterprise console, and are doing host-based AV, you may also have records of this host's activity in relation to virus eradication and possibly even Malware or Spyware detection. The last category is an emerging trend in host-based attacks from the Web, where malicious programs are downloaded to your corporate hosts or clients that are not normally detected through standard antivirus detection signatures. This has led to specialized antispyware tools that come with client software, as well as an enterprise management console that not only distributes updates, but can record when clients detect and eradicate one of these Malware programs. This is yet another tool that could be a contributor to your enterprise logging system, and can be potentially key in your forensics investigations. Now back to our investigation, where you are looking across all your logs collected from your various sources for the suspect IP address.

Up to this point your "circle" of investigation is just against the suspected host IP address, which may give you some data related to the suspected breach. But what if it turns up nothing abnormal or very little data at all? Now is the time that the forensics team needs to open up their investigation to a broader concentric circle of potential evidence. Again using the IP address of the suspected host, you may now broaden your search beyond the fourth octet, and back it up to the whole address range segment on which the suspect host resides. Now you will get a broader set of log activity, and will have to do some true analysis, as the record count may increase for the logged events, access denies, AV activity, log-ons, and so on, depending on your collection sources. At least now you are getting additional log data that may or may not be related. It was captured in the vicinity of the suspect host and may provide clues as to when the breach occurred by increased traffic patterns on that IP address range or segment. And you have data over a period of time, beyond just 24 hours worth, as you recall how our system was set up to collect and keep these audit logs for a period of time, and not just let it allow these log records to be overwritten.

You can now use this data, which may be volumes because you are collecting everything logged pertaining to an address range. You can now start with a basic trend analysis. As an example, you would pull the data for this segment by 24-hour time slices. Then do a metrics count on how many records were cut or collected for this period of time. Execute this trend analysis for 7, 14, or 21 days, to try to set a pattern of activity on this segment. If you are indeed dealing with an actual breach of the system, you may see an increase of activity just prior to the breach as access activity, or plain old "discovery" activity is increasing and your systems may have been cutting an increased number of log records, but nothing so specific as to set off alarms. You may now have a trend showing this increase across all systems or some system located within the suspect address range.

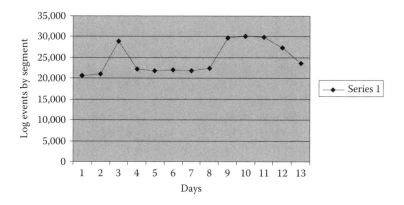

**Figure 8.1   Audit log record count by segment**

On the days where you see an abnormal increase in records, your forensics team would then begin sifting through the records specific to the day, to attempt to determine what caused the increase in log records. It is also very common to see increases in activity followed by some period of lull and then an increase again when the actual attack, breach, or worm launch occurs. This has been the case in after-the-fact investigations of known worm outbreaks such the Slammer worm, which propagated via UDB port 1434. When forensic investigators went back through Internet records, and did a specific search on port 1434 activity, they of course did indeed find it go "off the charts" in utilization on the day of its known outbreak. But further checks prior to that indicated that it was released well beforehand, but in much smaller numbers, as there were spikes in activity for that port but not so much as to draw attention. The belief is that possibly it was being "tested" at these times.

The point though, is that there was detectable traffic before the major release of a malicious worm or even attack, so as your analysts are going through your log analysis over the suspect segment, any aberrations even if they occur before the event, should be further investigated, as it is a common trait to see these increased traffic loads. Figure 8.1 illustrates a hypothetical traffic pattern analysis for two weeks worth of traffic on a segment being investigated.

By just running a report on your system for all log events from whatever sources you may have collected over that segment, you can get a similar audit log record count for a particular segment. In Figure 8.1, what we see is a common daily log number around 20,000 records or events, with some exceptions. Assuming the analysis team runs this report over this same segment for an even broader time period and does find that the

20,000 log records are the common daily average, then the dates of the 3rd and 9th through the 12th are suspect as they seem to exceed the 20,000 average. And for the sake of example, if the suspected breach occurred on or about the 10th, then this would fit the pattern of such an attack, in that there may have been malicious "discovery" work on this segment on the 3rd, but not so much as to set off any alarms, and then the refined or actual attack could have occurred on the 9th or 10th, hence the increased traffic and now the follow-on investigation.

Now you can focus on when this trend increase first started (the 3rd) and then drill down into the specifics, what changes, what new records were beginning to occur, and on what systems. Going further into the forensics of these logs will require that you be directly aware of the specific systems you are collecting records from and have the ability to drill down into these records for the purpose of this investigation. It will depend on the nature of the systems that you are collecting logs from as well as who to call in to assist in this forensics investigation. If you included log records from your intrusion prevention system, then it may warrant subject matter experts specific to this area or product tool. If the record increase is coming from one of your authentication systems, then that is merely an analyst most familiar with these systems and your enterprise. The trigger clue here is the increased records, then the source that generated them, and, hopefully, some specifics that can be garnered from these increased record counts which will lead to a more pinpointed source (another host, person, or credential, or possibly even program process). The trail may lead your investigators well outside your target logging zone or environment, but at least you will have some degree of sound data to go on and continue the investigation, even if it goes beyond your initial environment.

Without going into too much more detail, it should soon become evident that your system can provide all of this, with the right collection sources incorporated and investigation tools in the form of reports and ad hoc query capability. We got here by the fact that we needed to show the ability to maintain compliance to various regulations some of which are targeted for the protection of NPI data and the ability to determine whether our system is secure and has maintained its security controls utilizing the tool that you built. The whole area of computer forensics is a growing field, and there is a variety of reference sources available; we only touch on it here, as the tool that you will build can become one of the main components of your corporate computer forensics program. This was merely a simplistic example of how this tool can be put to use for conducting a forensics investigation. There is much more involved when investigating a large-scale breach or worm attack, but this should give you, the reader, an idea of how your systems can serve as a key component and make more of a selling point of how your enterprise can benefit from its implementation.

## Gaining Buy-In for Your System

This previous example provided one more justifiable reason for putting an enterprise log consolidation program into place, but even with all this evidence on why it is needed, you will still find pockets of resistance from within your organization. These areas of resistance may come from the stakeholders or owners of some of the very systems that you plan to collect data from in the first place.

The owners of these systems may see your system as the "beginning of the end," and feel threatened by the overarching size of your system and impact on their livelihood, and feel that their individual management of their systems gives them a key point of existence within the organization. This should be dismissed easily as most systems do have a place in the infrastructure, but may not warrant individual logging collection and review. We do believe there is economy in numbers and clear benefit in correlation. It might be time to work on a cost-benefit analysis on doing log collection individually versus doing it in a collective state. A very simplistic formula follows that could be utilized to make this point. It attempts to attach a dollar figure to events reported, and base it on the cost of that individual system. In the financial world and many business aspects there is a "cost per transaction, cost per mile flown," and the like. We are just trying to illustrate this in a similar manner to justify our consolidated system, spreading the investment out among all the systems, and reducing the hours spent on any single individual system. As you approach some of the target contributors to your log consolidation system, you can use one of our simple costing formulas that attempt to attach a "cost per event" to the system to illustrate both what they may be paying now for conducting their own log reviews and retention versus using a consolidated system. Where the following values are gathered as part of a survey and costing illustration, you can come up with a high-level estimate of cost per event on a monthly basis. This can be done with the following variables and equation:

$E$ = Number of relevant reported events per month from this device
$PMC$ = Annual product maintenance cost
$HRS$ = Hours per month required to monitor and maintain the system (may come from two sources: server or project support, and the security monitoring team/personnel)
$LR$ = Fully loaded labor rate

Plugging these figures into the following equation gives:

(PMC/12) + (HRS × LR)/E = Cost Per Detected Event

Running an example on a server tool might come up with the following costs:

E = 14 relevant or actionable security events reported
PMC = $22,000 annually
HRS = 50 (1.5 hours/day (30 days), 7 days week, + 5 hours/month for server and application support)
LR = $150.00 (fully burdened labor rate with overhead)

$$(PMC/12) + (HRS \times LR)/E$$

((22,000/12) + (50 × 150))/14 = $666.00 approximate cost per reported relevant event from this device

If the figures are close to accurate, this can give a low-level benchmark for cost of the device and the information it is providing. (Although this doesn't include the initial software outlay, as well as the hardware cost, as these will vary depending on how long the device has been on site, depreciation, and the like, so in order to remove these variables, these costs have been removed from the equation.) And again remember this exercise is high level, to further show the costs of supporting that device on an independent logging, review, and reporting level, versus the consolidated system toward which you are working.

So now you have a cost per event, and have to look at the event and determine how relevant and valuable to your security infrastructure it is; maybe it is well worth the $666 per event that it is reporting and protecting your environment as it stands today. However, by showing how your system can eliminate individual hours of monitoring and logging by system, the new cost to the organization comes in much lower as the 45 hours spent on their own system log reviews would be absorbed into your centralized system, the concept being that your centralized system would provide a more rules-based and automated system, so only a portion of these 45 hours (1.5/day × 30 days) would be rolled up into the centralized system. Also, by using their hour estimates on what they conduct on this process (and it is hoped they provide realistic hours), they may even be surprised at what it is costing them in hours and support costs to maintain compliance on their systems for corporate audit logging. The hope here is that they recognize the costs of how they are doing it now, and can see value in consolidating their logging and monitoring into the centralized system.

It will be important to get buy-in from the target systems that you plan to incorporate into your log consolidation system, as this will build your case for achieving the necessary start-up funding to execute your plan. As we stated going into this exercise, the target was to obtain a COTS system from the many market offerings that could easily be integrated into your environment to provide a much stronger security logging and monitoring presence across your enterprise. But the cost of such an adventure has to be justified, and this low-level approach from the target sources has been proven as one method to approach upper management with, and that is the greater the number of positive and supportive stakeholders, the better the chance of achieving funding.

Another area of stakeholders beyond the target system owners would be the compliance office, as we've already mentioned this tool fits neatly into your compliance architecture and strategy, possibly not as the single component but rather as a supporting component. So as stakeholders go, this one (the Compliance Officer), may not have individual systems, but from a regulatory perspective, he or she would clearly be listed as a stakeholder and should be approached when making your project plans and funding proposals.

Other potential stakeholders could come from the systems management arena, as you may find you are collecting far more data than they get with their mere alarms and alerts (SNMP, for example), and thus your proposed system could benefit their processes by adding more detail. This would take a degree of analysis with them, and possibly some form of demonstration or mockup of your system to show the value, but with your target COTS vendor's assistance this is usually an easily prepared exercise. And with this successful demonstration, you may gain yet another advocate of your project proposal to senior management for an enterprise audit log consolidation system.

After getting buy-in at the distributed levels, you may be nearly prepared to approach senior management, although it can take more than just a proposal paper and the previously listed advocates of your system. Many times a full business case may need to be assembled, which not only touts the technical merits of your system, the cost-benefit analysis, but also should very clearly call out the multiple drivers of this proposal. We have already covered, but warrant listing again, the drivers for your proposal. These drivers are more than just a proposal to create an improvement of your internal audit logging and monitoring processes, but also come from external influences, most specifically the regulatory side. The fact that your company is facing a growing number of regulations that require specific controls be in place, and that there be evidence of these controls during the course of an audit, your system can be shown to support these requirements. And it can't be denied that the regulatory environment is growing, with no relief in sight, so any tool or component that can ease the work to gain or maintain compliance is well worth the investment (and one hopes that as part of your business case, you can make this point).

The next obvious addition to your business case, or even basic project proposal, is the dollar cost advantages of a consolidated system over a distributed audit log monitoring system. We have covered various modeling methods in which costs are captured and compared between the two approaches, so it would be worthwhile to take one or more of these, attempt to capture your specific environment variables (number of servers to be consolidated, hours spent maintaining their individual audit logging methods, your software and manpower cost estimates) and see how these cost models depict the costs of managing your current audit logging processes.

The other cost that we have yet to discuss in much depth, mostly due to the fact is that it is one of the most difficult to capture, is what possible costs are associated with not putting into place your proposal. One portion of this cost you may be able to capture once you do the analysis of your target systems, and that is the cost of what your processes are today, that is, if they are being appropriately executed. The other side of this cost figure is the potential cost to the company if you are audited and found not to be compliant in proving your system controls to one of the governing regulatory agencies. There may be a defined fine for noncompliance that you can capture, but there is also the risk to business reputation, and possibly more for public companies, where consumer confidence and even business might drop due to publicized noncompliance. These costs are much more difficult to estimate and may vary by industry and company models, but suffice it to say, there is a cost of noncompliance, and if your initial study finds that your audit logging, monitoring, and controls are not in place, this can be a very high probability of costing the company sometime in the future.

All this preparation of your plan for gaining funding, approval, or recognition of your project prior to moving forward is well worth the effort (especially if you do have to go through this routine just to gain your basic funding). In today's corporate world, experience has shown that there are many agendas in the IT space no matter what the size of the company, so this effort, once mastered, can only make your project that much more effective from the very start.

Figure 8.2 illustrates some of these layers of the business where your project should be vetted in order to be prepared for your final presentation,

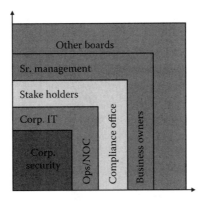

**Figure 8.2   Corporate stakeholders**

request, or approval from senior management. This is not necessarily a comprehensive list, but rather an outline sample of the layers that you should consider in order to put your plan into place, as all organizations (I use that term loosely) vary in their layers of control and approval cycles.

So by now, you either have done all the preparation work on your project proposal and plan to go forward, or you may have figured out the complexity of this project and decided "the old system isn't that bad." One would hope you have done this work and seen the true benefit to the organization and have made the decision to do your proposal, and possibly even the requisite business case, covering at least the topics contained herein, and have gained user acceptance from the various involved parties across your organization. Now comes the moment of truth: going in front of whatever corporate board or senior management group to gain the approval to execute, or possibly the approval to spend the estimated funding to initiate the project. The data contained here, as well as your own work to vet the proposal among your peers and stakeholders, will make the probability of success and gaining approval realistic.

# Future Implementation Strategies and Value-Added Components

We have now covered a variety of factors to help you justify moving forward with your consolidated logging architecture, and real-world returns to your enterprise today, but there is a whole other area of additional value-added features that could be incorporated into your system. Up to this point we have discussed what it can do with the data that you have within your enterprise, data you are already generating and have distributed across your network from a variety of devices. All of it can be very valuable data, and even more valuable when combined and correlated, and reports generated from this aggregation as we have pointed out. But this data is from your internal in-house systems, and is merely generated at a point in time. We have constructed it to glean some value from it, but we are still just dealing with mere log data. How can we make it even more valuable to the enterprise for any or all of the aspects we are using it for up to this point (attack profiling, alerting, early warning systems, and computer forensics)?

Here we point out a few methods you can use to potentially garner more value from this data by incorporating additional external data not inherent in your enterprise today. The first example would be to import a relatively new data source, the geographic location databases of IP addresses. There is actually a market developing that can provide a relation between IP address and geographic location, or geolocation capabilities. By taking a single IP address or range of addresses, there are firms that can provide databases that will pinpoint the address to a country, state, province, city, or region with some degree of accuracy. These are sub-scription-based services because the data is in need of constant updates, but worthy of the fee for a large enterprise capable of taking advantage of these inputs.

One such example may be to incorporate this geolocation data on Level One Alerts, that have a high confidence factor that they are not false positives. When displaying such alerts, instead of merely displaying the source address or addresses, a quick query of the geolocation database by this IP may identify the source as an off-shore location. It is common knowledge that many attacks are based off-shore due to belief that they can extend themselves beyond the United States' and developed countries' cyber-crime laws and therefore they position their attacks from off-shore locations. This type of data can further assist you in refining the threat level you may be facing, once you have a confidence level in the reliability of these geolocation databases. They can also assist in analyzing threats that may appear to be different, but with a geolocation determination, you may find that a group of attacks is all coming from one location, but from a variety of apparently different IP addresses. This could be the case where a student from a foreign university is launching the attack and has the knowledge to know not to launch it from any one IP or range of IP addresses, but rather use a multitude of address ranges, which would readily be available at any large university campus. The inputs from an accurate geolocation database would put it into perspective for all the various addresses that seem to be independently attacking your enterprise and showing up in your log consolidation system. This common factor can now be determined by geographic location through the use of this external input to your system.

It should become obvious that this type of input could clearly enhance the value of your reports and provide an additional discriminator in identifying attacks and possible sources. These types of geolocation databases are becoming more popular with a couple of commercial offerings now available on a subscription basis. Their initial marketing focus was on Web sales and formulating customer attention based on the incoming customer's location. Only recently has the security community begun looking to incorporate this data with attack data to better hone their security report accuracy. Thus, here is yet another requirement for your selection of a COTS reporting system, "Does the system allow for external data inputs or API calls to external data sources" (the data source being the geolocation database or source data).

The author actually built such a system with an early entry into the marketplace, Quova, which still offers this data on a subscription basis as well as simple methods to make calls to their database. It proved quite valuable to be able to gain insight to the locations from which suspected attacks were originating on all external firewalls being monitored, correlated, and reported across the enterprise. In fact, more than once it indicated cases where multiple scans were occurring on an East Coast firewall, and on the West Coast firewall, but they clearly were from different ranges of IP addresses, so they didn't appear to be the same originator. But when fed into the geolocation database, their source was identified as coming from the same province and country, at similar timeframes (actually one scan came first, followed by the next address range, but from the same province). This was deemed as not coincidental but probably a concerted scan against multiple outward facing points of one company, done by a single originator, but one that was trying to hide his identity by either assuming or coming from actual different IP address ranges. But the point here is that the geolocation database was able to pinpoint it as actually coming from co-located areas within one country. Thus, this add-on is just one more minor tool in the professional hacker tracker's toolkit or as emerging terminology is referring to it, an "Attack Management Console." (It's interesting to note that the security vendor community is constantly updating their terminology for our security toolkits; it wasn't long ago that the big "Threat Management Console" was put into place to counter the "Information Warfare" challenge facing the security professionals of the day.)

As today's security tools progress, it is expected that they will further incorporate many of these external sources such as geolocation which may become a standard offering either in the SIM/SEM product offerings, or as an add-on option in future versions. (The author's implementation of the Quova geolocation database was a custom-coded design, as there were no commercial SIM offerings available that incorporated this data feed out of the box.)

The point here though, is to implement a system that is not just tied to localized inputs but can also take in external inputs from a trusted source, such as the geolocation database as described herein. The rules engine for creating reports must also be able to take advantage of these external sources, as this would most likely be one of the points of making the accesses and correlation between the internal data and the external source and including it in your output reports. Another area of your tool that you may also want to utilize would be from external data feeds, would be for an alarming and alerting component if you choose to include that in your implementation. The next area shows how this can be helpful in your real-time reporting (and after the fact batch reports as well).

Another external source that is already incorporated into many correlation products is reference points to the CVE (common vulnerability exposures) values now associated with many security alerts. CVE values are a standardized list of names for vulnerabilities and other information security attributes.[1] This database is not intended merely as a lookup-type database, but rather as a common baseline for applications to share data on vulnerabilities across other databases and security tools. But these tools must agree to utilize the CVE database as the baseline, with its common numbering and labeling scheme for all vulnerabilities that it has classified for the common sharing to occur.

This is where your product analysis comes into play and you will need to identify the ability of your COTS tool to take advantage and supply APIs to the CVE values, yet another external data source, but definitely one that can add value to your correlation and reporting tool. The reference would be a "CVE Compatible" tool, which means it has the ability to share, read, and output CVE compatible vulnerability names. The result would be a system that would be able to share common vulnerability names, and vulnerability "ratings," which is based on set values. This alone provides value to your system, but the next step may be to gain insight to others' work in this area by sharing your output values or rather number of CVE types with external organizations. From a very simplistic view, this would provide you with the ability to compare hits on your systems by these values and compare these numbers with others, maybe even if only in a one-way viewpoint, where you go out and look up what common values are being recorded in other systems.

An example may be the Internet carriers who also have monitoring and detection systems in place and are reporting by CVE value the most common hits or signatures they see going across the Internet backbone.

By making this available you can cross-compare what you are seeing, or get another type of early warning system from them on what to look for on your perimeter. If your system has the appropriate rules engine for your reporting of the data that you collect, you could even put in a Level One or Level Two Alert preprogrammed for high-hitting CVE values that your carriers may have reported on, that may be headed your way, or may already be bouncing off your perimeter firewalls. Again this shows the importance of knowing what to look for in a COTS log consolidation product, to be able to incorporate these features into your system as it matures.

Another usage of CVE values may occur if you end up implementing independent logging systems, due to business unit organization, country segregation, or other political means. By incorporating CVE values on your detected vulnerabilities on each system, you could do a quick cross-comparison among these independent systems via a simple summary report from each. I know our whole purpose here was to build a single audit log consolidation system, but in the truly global enterprise, this may not be possible due to the sheer overall size, so there may have to be multiple systems, operating somewhat autonomously. With rollup reporting via CVE values, you could easily run a cross-comparison among these seemingly autonomous systems.

An example of this sharing could be when DDoS attacks are detected on your CISCO PIX firewalls. You may want to try to determine whether this is common across your enterprise and possibly out in the wild (the global Internet), but how does your system report this in a common manner? With CVE values, one type of value that identifies a Cisco firewall vulnerability equates to a CVE-2001-0375 string (see http://cve.mitre.org). If your logging system has multiple instances (say one per continent and thus no single repository, but very large repositories on each continent), then this value could be rolled up with a summary number of events and then shared among the distributed collection systems. Similar to the geolocation database identifier, the CVE value can provide you with a common key field to cross-compare among your various systems, and this is especially important if for some reason you have disparate systems (which can be the case in very large global enterprise systems). And taking this a step further, if you did incorporate the geolocation database, you may now find that your perimeter is getting attacked on multiple continents by the same attack type and from the same geolocation. You could only determine this if you had incorporated both of these external sources and were truly correlating all this data up to a single source either all at once or across your systems in a two-phased approach (first collecting and correlating it on each continent's logging system, and then rolling it up to some central reporting system). Figure 8.3 illustrates this approach for reporting and rollup.

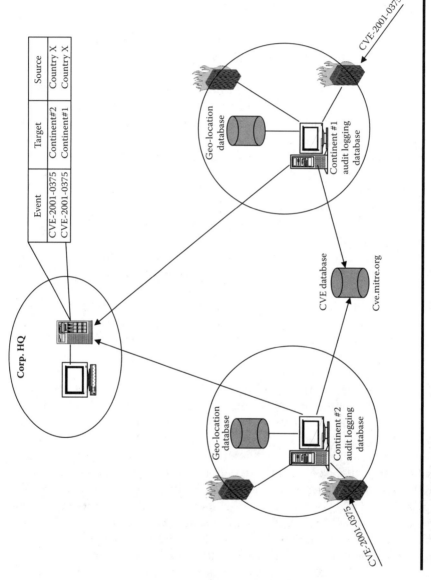

**Figure 8.3   Rollup reporting of CVEs and geolocation**

The diagram depicts how somewhat independent recording systems on different continents for one enterprise can capture events locally, do their own geolocation lookup, and CVE lookup, and then provide a rollup to a centralized station that would sort by CVE value and where commonalities existed, report on them to a central site. This rollup can then be reported at the HQ showing these potentially coordinated attacks against your enterprise, which can then be further analyzed and possibly have risk mitigation safeguards put into place. In this example, we have logging systems on Continent #1 and Continent #2. Both have logging of their perimeter firewalls consolidated into localized databases with lookups to the CVE value. These lookups have determined a common value of CVE-2001-0375 and when analyzed with a geolocation database found to be originating from the same country (by example Country X). By rolling these common values up to one centralized server/database, they can be correlated and found to be common hits, from a common geographic location. These commonalities or relationships could not have been determined if it weren't for the use of the CVE values, as well as the geolocation, and the further correlation up to the high-level repository (which isn't intended to capture the full data record, but more of the alerts, when common values are identified.

The potential use for CVE values will only grow as the industry tools adopt this standard, which appears to be the case as many SIM tools utilize this vulnerability classification structure. These "futures," the incorporation of external data sources, are actually coming into play today with many of the COTS products that you will be looking at for your consolidated logging toolkit (or attack management system). These were just two examples of external data sources; as the market evolves there will most likely be other useful external data sources or even correlation engines that will emerge that your system should be prepared to take advantage. The important thing is that your system is flexible enough to handle them. This ability to adapt will depend on the functions you require when evaluating these systems and it is hoped that this writing has given you the technical insight to identify how they apply to your environment.

So from here, you now have a very good handle on what can be accomplished with a consolidated audit logging architecture, the breadth of its uses, and benefits to your enterprise. The practices outlined are based on actual implementations in a global environment and should provide the reader with a strong foundation for evaluating and implementing any one of the strong COTS products in the marketplace today. So take these directions to heart, look deeply into your operating environment, and take the initiative to improve your overall security posture by applying this valuable toolset.

# Note

1. http://cve.mitre.org/ "Common Vulnerabilities and Exposures," January 2005.

# Index

**161**